G-5654

Hymns for the Gospels

GIA Publications, Inc.

Compiled and edited by W. Thomas Smith and
Robert J. Batastini

Music engraving by Philip Roberts; cover design
by Yolanda Durán

ISBN 1-57999-158-0

1 2 3 4 5 6 7 8 9 0

PREFACE

Until the time of Isaac Watts, congregational song consisted primarily of psalm singing. Without suggesting that psalm singing should be set aside, Watts, nonetheless, recognized psalmody as the hymnody of the Jewish covenant and called for a new hymnody that would reflect the Christian experience. His prolific output of new hymns thus gave birth to our present concept of hymnody: the product of human creativity inspired by, based upon, or in direct paraphrase of sacred scripture.

In many ways, a well-conceived hymn plays the same role as that of the homily, albeit more concise. It strives to break open the word of God, helping to apply it to the present, and helping to formulate the assembly's response. It has been said that in worship we proclaim the word of God, we preach the word of God, and in our hymnody, we sing the word of God. Martin Luther said that the congregation shared the word of God with each other in their hymn singing, and a contemporary colleague, Virgil C. Funk, has suggested that in hymn singing, the assembly claims the word of God.

The Second Vatican Council of the Roman Catholic Church led to the development of the three-year Lectionary of Sunday readings. The adoption of that Lectionary across denominational lines prompted contemporary hymn writers—mostly Protestant—to address the significant increase in the amount of scripture read in Sunday worship. The creative outpouring which occurred has come to be known as the "hymn explosion" of the final third of the 20th century. This creative energy continues to emerge from an ever-growing number of gifted contemporary hymn writers.

In this volume the editors have endeavored to give a new dimension to the "hymn of the day" concept. We began by identifying all of the gospel passages read on the Sundays of the three-year cycle of readings, accommodating the variants among different versions of the Lectionary. We then sifted through the works of a wide range of contemporary hymn writers seeking a hymn for each gospel passage. While always evaluating the quality of the poetry itself—attempting to use only the best, we gave first preference to texts based entirely on the specific passage. When a such was not found, we searched for a more general hymn especially suited to the topic of the particular gospel. In all but one or two cases, we have succeeded—we believe—in finding a suitable hymn of the day drawn exclusively from the output of today's hymn writers.

Finally, lest the whole exercise become academic by requiring congregations to navigate a new and unfamiliar tune each week, most of the texts in this collection have been set to familiar tunes to accommodate instant accessibility.

W. Thomas Smith
Retired Executive Director of the Hymn
Society in the United States and Canada

Robert J. Batastini
Past President of the Hymn Society, Senior
Editor of GIA Publications, Inc.

This collection sets out to provide a suitable hymn for each Sunday of the three-year Lectionary, based on the gospel reading. To determine the hymn for a particular day, simply look up the citation for that day's gospel reading in the index below. For the most part, these hymns have been set to familiar tunes to make them accessible on a week after week basis.

MATTHEW

Mark

Luke

JOHN

Make Our Church One Joyful Choir   1

1. Make our church one joy-ful choir On this glad and fes-tive day And by song in-voke the fire That in-vites our hearts to pray:
2. Bend us low by song and prayer, Low e-nough to lift the cross And to take the weight and bear Love's un-count-ed fi-nal cost.
3. Lift us up by song and prayer Till the way we deal with loss And our acts and words of care Trace the pat-tern of your cross:
4. Bend us, lift us, make us strong, Send us out with wind and fire, So the world may hear the song That we of-fer as your choir:

Shape us, Christ, to live and claim All it means to bear your name.

Text: Thomas H. Troeger, b.1945, © 1994, Oxford University Press, Inc.
Tune: DIX, 7 7 7 7 77; arr. from Conrad Kocher, 1786-1872, by William H. Monk, 1823-1889

2 The Kingdom of God

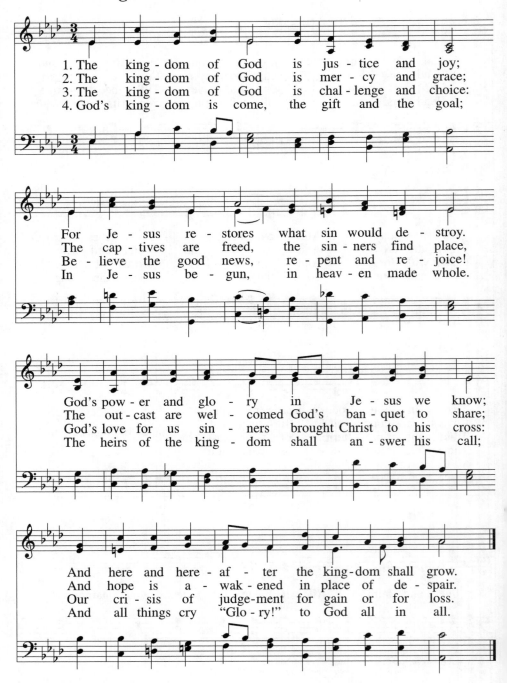

1. The king-dom of God is jus-tice and joy;
   For Je - sus re - stores what sin would de - stroy.
   God's pow - er and glo - ry in Je - sus we know;
   And here and here - af - ter the king-dom shall grow.

2. The king-dom of God is mer - cy and grace;
   The cap - tives are freed, the sin - ners find place,
   The out-cast are wel - comed God's ban - quet to share;
   And hope is a - wak-ened in place of de - spair.

3. The king-dom of God is chal - lenge and choice:
   Be - lieve the good news, re - pent and re - joice!
   God's love for us sin - ners brought Christ to his cross:
   Our cri - sis of judge-ment for gain or for loss.

4. God's king - dom is come, the gift and the goal;
   In Je - sus be - gun, in heav - en made whole.
   The heirs of the king - dom shall an - swer his call;
   And all things cry "Glo - ry!" to God all in all.

Text: Bryn A. Rees, 1911-1983, © Mrs. Olwen Scott
Tune: LAUDATE DOMINUM , 10 10 11 11; Charles H. H. Parry, 1848-1918

1. The scant - est touch of grace can heal A
2. Ob - serve a hand stretched out to brush The
3. She can - not see the Sav - ior's face, But
4. Like her, O Christ, we reach for you. One

wound that's bled for years If first we dare to
hem of Je - sus' gown. That bleed - ing wom - an
lung - es for his robe: At once a surge of
touch is all we need. We stretch for grace to

reach and feel Be - yond our pain and tears.
trusts one touch Will make her bod - y sound.
heal - ing grace Where stub - born blood has flowed.
make us new And heal our wounds that bleed.

Text: Thomas H. Troeger, b.1945, © 1994, Oxford University Press, Inc.
Tune: DETROIT, CM; Supplement to *Kentucky Harmony*, 1820; harm. by Gerald H. Knight, 1908-1979, © The Royal School of Church Music

4 When Our Confidence Is Shaken

unison

1. When our con - fi - dence is shak - en
2. So - lar sys - tems, void of mean - ing,
3. In the dis - ci - pline of pray - ing,
4. God is love; and he re - deems us

In be - liefs we thought se - cure;
Freeze the spir - it in - to stone;
When its hard - est to be - lieve;
In the Christ we cru - ci - fy:

When the spir - it in its sick - ness
Al - ways our re - search - es lead us
In the drudg - er - y of car - ing,
This is God's e - ter - nal an - swer

Seeks but can - not find a cure:
To the ul - ti - mate Un - known:
When it's not e - nough to grieve:
To the world's e - ter - nal why;

God is ac - tive in the ten - sions
Faith must die, or come full cir - cle
Faith ma - tur - ing, learns ac - cept - ance
May we in this faith ma - tur - ing

Of a faith not yet ma - ture.
To its source in God a - lone.
Of the in - sights we re - ceive.
Be con - tent to live and die.

Text: Fred Pratt Green, 1903-2000, © 1971, Hope Publishing Co.
Tune: PICARDY, 8 7 8 7 8 7; French Carol; harm. by Richard Proulx, b.1937, © 1986, GIA Publications, Inc.

5 Lord Christ, When First You Came to Earth

1. Lord Christ, when first you came to earth, Up-
2. O awe-some Love, which finds no room In
3. New ad-vent of the love of Christ, Will
4. O wound-ed hands of Je-sus, build In

on a cross they bound you. And
life where sin de - nies you. And,
we a - gain re - fuse you. Till
us your new cre - a - tion: Our

mocked your sav - ing king-ship's worth By
doomed to death, shall bring to doom The
in the night of hate and war We
pride is dust, our boast-ing stilled; We

thorns with which they crowned you. And
pow'r which cru - ci - fies you, Till
per - ish as we lose you? From
wait your rev - e - la - tion. O

still   our wrongs   may   fash - ion now,   New
not   a   stone   be   left on stone,   And
an - cient doubts   our   minds re - lease   To
Love   that   tri - umphs   o - ver loss,   We

thorns to pierce   that   stead - y brow,   And
then   the   na - tion's   pride, o'er - thrown, Will
seek   the king - dom   of your peace,   By
bring our hearts   be - fore your cross   To

robe   of   sor - row   round   you.
nev - er - more   de - fy   you!
which a - lone   we   choose   you.
fin - ish your   sal - va - tion.

Text: W. Russel Bowie, 1882-1969, alt., ©
Tune: MIT FREUDEN ZART, 8 7 8 7 88 7; Bohemian Brethren's *Kirchengesang*, 1566

6 We Come, O Christ, to You

1. We come, O Christ, to you, True Son of God and man,
2. You are the Way to God, Your blood our ran-som paid;
3. You are the liv-ing Truth, All wis-dom dwells in you,
4. You on-ly are true Life— To know you is to live
5. We wor-ship you, Lord Christ, Our Sav-ior and our King;

By whom all things con - sist, In whom all life be - gan:
In you we face our judge And mak - er un - a - fraid.
The source of ev - 'ry skill, The one e - ter - nal TRUE!
The more a - bun - dant life That earth can nev - er give.
To you our youth and strength A - dor-ing - ly we bring;

In you a - lone we live and move,
Be - fore the throne ab - solved we stand:
O great I AM! In you we rest,
O ris - en Lord! We live in you:
So fill our hearts that all may view

And have our be - ing in your love.
Your love has met your law's de - mand.
Sure an - swer to our ev - 'ry quest.
In us each day your life re - new!
Your life in us and turn to you!

Text: Margaret Clarkson, © 1957, renewed 1985, Hope Publishing Co.
Tune: DARWALL'S 148TH, 6 6 6 6 88; John Darwall, 1731-1789; harm. from *The Hymnal 1940*

Banned and Banished By Their Neighbors 7

1. Banned and banished by their neighbors, Full of sores, accused of sin, Scorned and scarred, the ten were calling, Warning all, "Unclean, Unclean!"

2. Jesus met them with compassion, Heard their cry, "Have mercy, Lord!" Cleansed their flesh and turned them homeward With his saving, healing Word.

3. Still, O Christ, we bring before you Ills of body, mind and soul. Speak again your Word of healing; Cleanse, renew and make us whole!

4. Then, redeemed, restored, forgiven, Lord, this other gift impart: For the mercy you have shown us, Grant us each a grateful heart.

Text: Herman G. Stuempfle, b.1923, © 1997, GIA Publications, Inc.
Tune: STUTTGART, 8 7 8 7; *Psalmodia Sacra*, 1715; adapt. and harm. by William Henry Havergal, 1793-1870, alt.

8 A Beggar-King Comes Riding

1. A beg-gar-king comes rid - ing To Ju-dah's roy - al
2. A home-less king comes rid - ing In - to Je-ru-sa -
3. An ex - ile-king comes rid - ing In - to Je-ru-sa -

town, His mount no pranc - ing stal - lion, Sharp
lem. The might - y rise a - gainst him To
lem. He claims no splen - did pal - ace, His

thorns his on - ly crown. A palm branch is his
mock him and con - demn. He ban - quets with the
grave a bor - rowed tomb. But from that tomb God

scep - ter, A don - key is his steed. His
out - cast Whom all the great de - spise, And
lifts him A - bove all crowns and kings, And

throne will be a cross - beam On which for us he'll bleed.
then up - on a hill - top With thieves he hangs and dies.
now to him, "Ho - san - na!" The whole cre - a - tion sings!

Text: Herman G. Stuempfle, b.1923, © 2000, GIA Publications, Inc.
Tune: PASSION CHORALE, 7 6 7 6 D; Hans Leo Hassler, 1564-1612; harm. by J. S. Bach, 1685-1750

Enter in the Realm of God   9

1. En - ter in the realm of God. It has come, and
2. In com - mu - ni - ties that serve, And a - mong the
3. God has loved, and so we love, And we give that
4. Come a - gain, O Christ, to rule In that realm that

yet will be. It is known, and yet un - known.
saints who care, There is jus - tice for the poor,
all may share In the heal - ing God sup - plies,
has no end. May your chil - dren ev - 'ry - where

Christ re - vealed to mys - ter - y.
And new free - dom from de - spair.
In good news that we de - clare.
Hear your greet - ing: "Wel - come, friend!"

Text: Lavon Bayler, b.1933, © 1994, The Pilgrim Press
Tune: HEINLEIN, 7 7 7 7; attr. to Martin Herbst, 1654-1681

1. One wed-ding dress long put a-way And one still to be worn— With God all things are pos-si-ble; Two ba-bies will be born.
2. To Mar-y, yet to be a bride, The an-gel Ga-briel came. With God all things are pos-si-ble; She hears her ba-by's name.
3. E-liz-a-beth so long for a wife— No moth-er-hood for her! With God all things are pos-si-ble; She feels her ba-by stir.
4. Like Mar-y, we wait for the day That says new life may come, And like E-liz'-beth find that day And hope for new life gone.
5. O God, with you we hear the name Of life un-planned and free— We feel the kick-ing of the life It seemed could nev-er be.
6. One wed-ding dress long put a-way And one still to be worn— With God all things are pos-si-ble; Two ba-bies will be born!

Text: Richard Leach, © 1996, Selah Publishing Co., Inc.
Tune: MORNING SONG, CM; Wyeth's *Repository of Sacred Music,* 1813; harm. by C. Winfred Douglas, 1867-1944

Lord, Whose Then Shall They Be 11

1. Lord, whose then shall they be, These treas-ured goods we store? Shall all the wealth we gain and guard Be-yond a day en-dure?
2. We trust earth's tran-sient gifts To feed and sat-is-fy, To form a rock on which to stand Un-til, at last, we die.
3. But noth-ing born of earth Un-shak-en can a-bide. Like sand it soon is swept a-way In time's swift, swirl-ing tide.
4. O Christ, who of-fered all, Teach us the truth a-gain: That on-ly what we give in love Shall through all time a-bide.
5. Help us to hold in trust The treas-ured goods we store And share them where you bid us serve The dis-pos-sessed and poor.

Text: Herman G. Stuempfle, b.1923, © 1997, GIA Publications, Inc.
Tune: SOUTHWELL, SM; Daman's *Psalmes*, 1579, alt.

12 When John Baptized by Jordan's River

1. When John bap - tized by Jor - dan's riv - er
2. There as the Lord, bap - tized and pray - ing,
3. O Son of Man, our na - ture shar - ing,

In faith and hope the peo - ple came,
Rose from the stream, the sin - less one,
In whose o - be - dience all are blest,

That John and Jor - dan might de - liv - er
A voice was heard from heav - en say - ing,
Sav - ior, our sins and sor - rows bear - ing,

Their trou - bled souls from sin and shame.
"This is my own be - lov - ed Son."
Hear us and grant us this re - quest:

They came to seek a new be - gin - ning,
There as the Fa - ther's word was spo - ken,
Dai - ly to grow, by grace de - fend - ed,

The hu - man spir - it's age - less quest,
Not in the pow'r of wind and flame,
Filled with the Spir - it from a - bove;

Re - pent - ance, and an end of sin - ning,
But of his love and peace the to - ken,
In Christ bap - tized, be - loved, be - friend - ed,

Re - nounc - ing ev - 'ry wrong con - fessed.
Seen as a dove, the Spir - it came.
Chil - dren of God in peace and love.

Text: Timothy Dudley-Smith, b.1926, © 1984, Hope Publishing Co.
Tune: RENDEZ À DIEU, 9 8 9 8 D; Louis Bourgeois, c.1510-1561

13 Let Your Spirit Teach Me, Lord

1. Let your Spir - it teach me, Lord,
2. Touch my eyes, that I may see
3. Touch my mind to un - der - stand
4. Touch my lips to tell a - broad

As I bow be - fore your Word;
All the truth you have for me;
All that you for me have planned;
All the grace and truth of God;

Au - thor of the sa - cred page,
Here with - in your writ - ten Word
Help me find my hum - ble place
Let my life a - dorn my word—

All my be - ing now en - gage.
May I find my liv - ing Lord.
In your pur - pos - es of grace.
On - ly Christ be seen and heard.

I am dark - ness, you are light:
Touch my heart, that I may learn
Touch my will, that I may bow
Let your Spir - it teach me now,

Quick - en now my in - ward sight;
For your ho - li - ness to yearn;
To the truth you give me now;
As be - fore your Word I bow;

Let your Spir - it's grace be giv'n;
Kin - dle there your deep de - sire
Help me walk the pil - grim way
With your ho - ly ful - ness fill,

Break to me the Bread of heav'n.
For a life made pure by fire.
In o - be - dience day by day.
Work in me your per - fect will.

Text: Margaret Clarkson, © 1962. Renewed 1990 by Hope Publishing Co.
Tune: SALZBURG, 7 7 77 D; Jakob Hintze, 1622-1702; harm. by J.S. Bach, 1685-1750

14   The Sun Was Bright that Easter Dawn

1. The sun was bright that Easter dawn; Alleluia! Alleluia! But brighter still the risen Son! Alleluia! Alleluia!
2. The women hurried to his tomb; Alleluia! Alleluia! But only found an empty room! Alleluia! Alleluia!
3. The sleeping birds awoke to sing Alleluia! Alleluia! In praise of Christ, their risen King! Alleluia! Alleluia!
4. Let trumpets add their joyous sound Alleluia! Alleluia! And anthems soar the world around! Alleluia! Alleluia!
5. And you, good Christian folk, rejoice! Alleluia! Alleluia! Sing out to him with heart and voice: "Alleluia! Alleluia!"
6. For Christ has conquered death's long night Alleluia! Alleluia! And shines in resurrection light! Alleluia! Alleluia!

Text: Herman G. Stuempfle, b.1923, © 1997, GIA Publications, Inc.
Tune: PUER NOBIS, LM; adapt. by Michael Praetorius, 1571-1621

1. You call to us, Lord Je - sus, As once in Gal - i - lee
2. You came to preach de - liv - 'rance, To set the cap - tives free,
3. You sum - mon us to vi - sions Of what this world can be,
4. The path you bid us fol - low Is not an eas - y road,

You called to James and An - drew, "Come now and fol - low me."
To heal the bro - ken - heart - ed, To make the sight - less see.
Of hope and peace and free - dom For all hu - man - i - ty.
And doubt or pain or con - flict Will some - times be our load.

They left their nets and fol - lowed, And did not look be - hind;
Your min - is - try of mer - cy And jus - tice is our task;
For jus - tice we will la - bor For ev - 'ry hu - man soul
Lord, grant us strength and cour - age To walk the way you trod,

Lord, we like them will fol - low, Our life in you to find.
Help us like true dis - ci - ples To do the work you ask.
Till greed and ha - tred van - ish, And hu - man - kind is whole.
Till we be - hold in glo - ry The ra - diant face of God.

Text: Joy F. Patterson, b.1931, © 1994, Hope Publishing Co.
Tune: AURELIA, 7 6 7 6 D; Samuel Sebastian Wesley, 1810-1876

16 Down Galilee's Slow Roadways

1. Down Gal - i - lee's slow road - ways A stran-ger trav-eled
2. A - ris - ing from the riv - er He saw the heav-ens
3. We too have found a road - way; It led us to this

on From Naz - a - reth to Jor - dan To
torn; It seemed the sky so o - pen Re -
place. We all have had to trav - el In

be bap - tised by John He went down to the
vealed the Spir - it's form. The ho - ly dove de -
search of hope and grace. But now be - side this

wa - ters Like sol - dier, scribe and slave, But
scend - ed A - mid a glo - rious voice: "You
wa - ter A - gain a voice is heard. "You

there with - in the riv - er The sign was birth and grave.
are my own be - lov - ed—My child, my heart, my choice."
are my own, my cho - sen, Be - lov - ed of your Lord."

Text: Sylvia Dunstan, 1955-1993, © 1991, GIA Publications, Inc.
Tune: LANCASHIRE, 7 6 7 6 D; Henry T. Smart, 1813-1879

Help Us Forgive, Forgiving Lord   17

1. Help us for - give, for - giv - ing Lord, The
2. For on the cross you bore for us The
3. Let grace un - lock each pris - oned heart, Un -
4. And then, the bro - ken cir - cle closed, The

wrong that oth - ers do And, when our hearts are
curse, the scorn, the hate And gave your life to
coil each fist - ed hand Un - til from hate our
bro - ken friend-ships healed, Lord, hold us fast with -

pierced by pain, To bring the hurt to you.
lift from us Sin's cruel and crush - ing weight.
hearts are freed, Our hands in love ex - tend.
in the bonds By your for - give - ness sealed.

Text: Herman G. Stuempfle, b.1923, © 1997, GIA Publications, Inc.
Tune: DETROIT, CM; Supplement to *Kentucky Harmony*, 1820; harm. by Gerald H. Knight, 1908-1979, © The Royal School of Church Music

18 Wild and Lone the Prophet's Voice

1. Wild and lone the proph - et's voice
2. "Bear the fruit re - pent - ance sows:
3. With such preach - ing stark and bold

Ech - oes through the des - ert still,
Lives of jus - tice, truth, and love.
John pro - claimed sal - va - tion near,

Call - ing us to make a choice,
Trust no oth - er claim than those;
And his time - less warn - ings hold

Bid - ding us to do God's will:
Set your heart on things a - bove.
Words of hope to all who hear.

"Turn from sin and be bap - tized;
Soon the Lord will come in pow'r,
So we dare to jour - ney on,

Cleanse your heart and mind and soul.
Burn - ing clean the thresh - ing floor:
Led by faith through ways un - trod,

Quit - ting all the sins you prized,
Then will flames the chaff de - vour;
Till we come at last like John

Yield your life to God's con - trol."
Wheat a - lone shall fill God's store."
To be - hold the Lamb of God.

Text: Carl P. Daw, Jr. b.1944, © 1989, Hope Publishing Co.
Tune: SALZBURG, 7 7 7 7 D; Jakob Hintze, 1622-1702; harm. by J.S. Bach, 1685-1750

19 God Whose Giving Knows No Ending

1. God, whose giv-ing knows no end-ing, From your rich and end-less store: Na-ture's won-der, Je-sus' wis-dom, Cost-ly cross, grave's shat-tered door, Gift-ed by you, we turn to you, Of-f'ring

2. Skills and time are ours for press-ing Toward the goals of Christ, your Son: All at peace in health and free-dom, Rac-es joined, the Church made one. Now di-rect our dai-ly la-bor, Lest we

3. Treas-ure, too, you have en-trust-ed, Gain through pow'rs your grace con-ferred; Ours to use for home and kin-dred, And to spread the Gos-pel Word. O-pen wide our hands in shar-ing, As we

up   our - selves in   praise;   Thank-ful   song shall rise   for -
strive   for   self   a - lone;   Born with   tal - ents, make   us
heed Christ's age - less   call,   Heal - ing,   teach-ing, and   re -

ev - er,   Gra - cious   do - nor of   our   days.
ser - vants Fit   to   an - swer at   your   throne.
claim - ing, Serv - ing   you   by   lov - ing   all.

Text: Robert L. Edwards, b.1915, © 1961, renewed 1989, The Hymn Society. Administered by Hope Publishing Co.
Tune: RUSTINGTON, 8 7 8 7 D; Charles H. Parry, 1848-1918

20   The Hands that First Held Mary's Child

1. The hands that first held Mar - y's child Were
2. When Jo - seph mar - veled at the size Of
3. "This child shall be Em - man - u - el, Not
4. The tools which Jo - seph laid a - side A

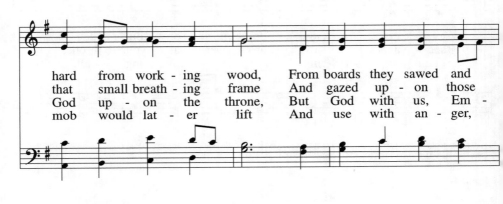

hard from work - ing wood, From boards they sawed and
that small breath - ing frame And gazed up - on those
God up - on the throne, But God with us, Em -
mob would lat - er lift And use with an - ger,

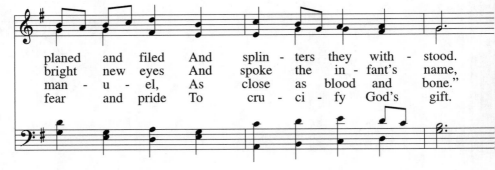

planed and filed And splin - ters they with - stood.
bright new eyes And spoke the in - fant's name,
man - u - el, As close as blood and bone."
fear and pride To cru - ci - fy God's gift.

This day   they gripped no   tool   of   steel,   They
The   an - gel's words he   once   had dreamed Poured
The   ti - ny   form   in   Jo - seph's palms Con -
Let   us,   O   Lord,   not   on - ly   hold   The

drove   no   i - ron   nail,   But   cra - dled from   the
down   from   heav - en's   height,   And   like   the   host   of
firmed   what   he   had   heard,   And   from   his   heart   rose
child   who's   born   to - day,   But   charged with   faith   may

head   to   heel   Our   Lord   new - born and   frail.
stars   that   beamed Blessed earth   with   wel - come   light.
hymns   and   psalms   For   heav - en's   hu - man   word.
we   be   bold   To   fol - low   in   his   way.

Text: Thomas H. Troeger, b.1945, © 1994, Oxford University Press, Inc.
Tune: FOREST GREEN, CMD; English; harm. by Ralph Vaughan Williams, 1872-1958, © Oxford University Press, Inc., alt.

21 The Virgin Mary Had a Baby Boy

1. The vir - gin Mar - y had a ba - by boy, The
2. The an - gels sang when the ba - by born, The
3. The wise men saw where the ba - by born, The

vir - gin Mar - y had a ba - by boy, The
an - gels sang when the ba - by born, The
wise men saw where the ba - by born, The

vir - gin Mar - y had a ba - by boy, And they
an - gels sang when the ba - by born, And they
wise men went where the ba - by born, And they

say that his name was Je - sus.
say that his name was Je - sus.
say that his name was Je - sus.

He come from the glo - ry, he come from the
glo - rious king-dom. Oh, yes! be-liev - er!
Oh, yes! be-liev - er! He come from the
glo - ry, he come from the glo - rious king-dom.

22 Lord, Teach Us How to Pray

1. Lord, teach us how to pray As once the twelve you taught, For we can nev-er find the words To praise you as we ought.

2. Lord, teach us how to pray When hearts are dull and dead, Or when we feel no thirst for you And faith, once firm, has fled.

3. Lord, teach us how to pray When cares dis-tract the mind. Help us to wait in qui-et-ness, A calm-er spir-it find.

4. Lord, teach us how to pray; Re-kin-dle faith's bright flame, Un-til our faith leaps up a-gain To speak and praise your name.

5. Lord, teach us how to pray; Re-mind us day by day That you wait ea-ger-ly to hear Be-fore we think to pray.

Text: Herman G. Stuempfle, b.1923, © 2000, GIA Publications, Inc.
Tune: ST. THOMAS, SM; Aaron Williams; harm. by Lowell Mason, 1792-1872

Eternal Spirit of the Living Christ 23

1. E - ter - nal Spir - it of the liv - ing Christ,
2. Come, pray in me the prayer I need this day;
3. Come with the strength I lack, bring vi - sion clear

I know not how to ask or what to say;
Help me to see your pur - pose and your will,
Of hu - man need; oh, give me eyes to see

I on - ly know my need, as deep as life,
Where I have failed, what I have done a - miss;
Ful - fill - ment of my life in love out - poured:

And on - ly you can teach me how to pray.
Held in for - giv - ing love, let me be still.
My life in you, O Christ; your love in me.

Text: Frank von Christierson, b.1900, © The Hymn Society. Administered by Hope Publishing Co.
Tune: EVENTIDE, 10 10 10 10; William H. Monk, 1823-1889, alt.; arr. by Evelyn Simpson-Curenton, b.1953, © 2000, GIA Publications, Inc.

24 Christ, the One Who Tells the Tale

1. Christ, the one who tells the tale Like-ning earth and heav-en, Christ, the son for whom the king Gives the wed-ding ban-quet, Christ, the slave who tells the guests Ev-'ry-thing is read-y, Je-sus,

2. Christ, made light of by the guests, Seized, mis-treat-ed, mur-dered, Christ, the death of death, the flame That will burn its cit-y, Christ, sent to the streets to call Ev-'ry-bod-y found there, Je-sus,

3. Christ, who fills the hall with guests, Good and bad to-geth-er, Christ, the wed-ding robe to wear For the king's in-spec-tion, Christ, the one who tells the tale Like-ning earth and heav-en, Je-sus,

rab - bi,   son and slave,   Mer - cy! Al - le - lu - ia!
vic - tim,   vic - tor, voice,   Mer - cy! Al - le - lu - ia!
net and   robe and friend, Mer - cy! Al - le - lu - ia!

Text: Richard Leach, © 1996, Selah Publishing Co., Inc.
Tune: ST. KEVIN, 7 6 7 6 D; Arthur Seymour Sullivan, 1872

The Branch that Bends with Clustered Fruit   25

1. The   branch   that bends with   clus - tered fruit Still
2. The   spin - dly, twist - ed,   tan - gled coil   Of
3. The   prun - er's hook will   gen - tly play   Where
4. O   God,   who fills with   rain and sun   The

needs the prun - er's blade To keep   it close to
branch - es o - ver - grown Pro - duc - es noth - ing
fruit - ful growth is seen But like an axe will
grapes we press for wine, Cut off the growth our

vine and root Or else its strength will fade.
from its toil But feeds it - self a - lone.
slash a - way The emp - ty net of green.
fears have spun And prune us to your vine.

Text: Thomas H. Troeger, b.1945, © 1994, Oxford University Press, Inc.
Tune: WINCHESTER OLD, CM; Thomas Est; harm. from *Hymns Ancient and Modern*, 1922

26 For God Risk Everything

1. For God risk ev-'ry-thing! Since ev-'ry-thing we
2. How shriv-eled, Lord, the soul That grips what it re-
3. From hearts that hide and hoard The treas-ures that you

own, Our laugh-ter, tears, the songs we sing, Our
ceives And dares not free its an-xious hold But
send Free us, till we by faith, O Lord, Shall

breath, our flesh and bone, Are no more ours to
fool-ish-ly be-lieves That you are too se-
act as you in-tend, Till we risk all for

keep Than wind that rush-es by Or dreams that flick-er
vere To par-don an-y loss, For-get-ting how your
you, Risk ev-'ry-thing you give, And risk-ing, learn what

in our sleep Or clouds that fade to sky.
son made clear For - give - ness on the cross.
Je - sus knew: By risk - ing all, we live.

Text: Thomas H. Troeger, b.1945, © 1996, Oxford University Press, Inc.
Tune: TERRA BEATA, SMD; English Melody; adapt. by Franklin L. Sheppard, 1852-1930

When You, Lord, Walked   27

1. When you, Lord, walked through Sab - bath fields Of
2. But fol - l'wing eyes watched ev - 'ry hand; The
3. Where, Sav - ior, do you walk to - day, Which
4. O Christ, when you walk through our fields Let

ris - ing, rip - ened grain, Your peo - ple ate the
scribes could not be - lieve That you would sim - ply
field or road or street? Whom do you touch a -
us be by your side To learn from those you've

gra - cious yield That filled their hearts a - gain.
change their ban To let the poor re - ceive.
long the way? What an - ger do you meet?
fed and healed The love that you pro - vide.

Text: Sylvia Dunstan, 1955-1993, © 1991, GIA Publications, Inc.
Tune: MORNING SONG, CM; Wyeth's *Repository of Sacred Music*, 1813; harm by C. Winfred Douglas, 1867-1944

28 The Moon with Borrowed Light

1. The moon with bor - rowed light Gives wit - ness to the
2. When tem - ple Le - vites asked What ti - tle did John
3. The clouds of sin yet mask Earth's tan - gled, stub - bly

sun, Dis - creet - ly fad - ing with the night When
claim, He said he had a sin - gle task A
ground, And O how man - y hearts still ask Where

morn - ing has be - gun. John's bor-rowed light was drawn From
sin - gle goal and aim: To re - di - rect their sight Be -
God's clear path is found. For bor-rowed light we pray So

heav - en's vi - brant rays, His life a wit - ness
yond what he had done To Christ the pure and
we may be a sign That points to Christ, the

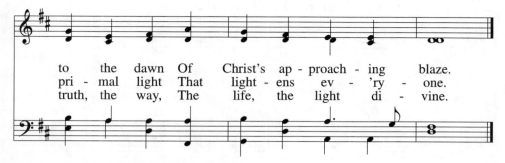

to the dawn Of Christ's ap - proach - ing blaze.
pri - mal light That light - ens ev - 'ry - one.
truth, the way, The life, the light di - vine.

Text: Thomas H. Troeger, b.1945, © 1994, Oxford University Press, Inc.
Tune: DIADEMATA, SMD; George J. Elvey, 1816-1893

Sing Praise to God for Friends   29

1. Sing praise to God for friends who bring Our
2. We may not see their fold - ed hands Nor
3. And do those clouds of wit - ness - es Whose
4. Sing praise for that great com - pa - ny Of

needs to Christ the Lord, Who pray that he will
know what prayers they raise, But Christ will al - ways
race has now been run Still lift their prayers by
all who in - ter - cede, Who by the hid - den

bend to us And speak his heal - ing Word.
hear the voice That for an - oth - er prays.
day and night For us be - fore God's throne?
hand of prayer Sup - port us in our need.

Text: Herman G. Stuempfle, b.1923, © 1997, GIA Publications, Inc.
Tune: AZMON, CM; Carl G. Gläser, 1784-1829; harm. by Lowell Mason, 1792-1872

30 As We Gather at Your Table

1. As we gath - er at your Ta - ble,
2. Turn our wor - ship in - to wit - ness
3. Gra - cious Spir - it, help us sum - mon

As we lis - ten to your Word,
In the sac - ra - ment your of life;
Oth - er guests to share that feast

Help us know, O God, your pres - ence:
Send us forth to love and serve you,
Where tri - um - phant Love will wel - come

Let our hearts and minds be stirred. Nour - ish us with
Bring - ing peace where there is strife. Give us, Christ, your
Those who had been last and least. There no more will

sa - cred sto - ry Till we claim it as our own;
great com - pas - sion To for - give as you for - gave;
en - vy blind us Nor will pride our peace de - stroy,

Teach us through this ho - ly ban - quet
May we still be - hold your im - age
As we join with saints and an - gels

How to make Love's vic - t'ry known.
In the world you died to save.
To re - peat the sound - ing joy.

Text: Carl P. Daw, Jr., b.1944, © 1989, Hope Publishing Co.
Tune: HOLY MANNA, 8 7 8 7 D; William Moore

31 God Has Spoken By His Prophets

1. God has spo - ken by his proph - ets, Spo - ken
2. God has spo - ken by Christ Je - sus, Christ, the
3. God is speak - ing by his Spir - it, Speak - ing

his un - chang-ing Word; Each from age to age pro - claim-ing
ev - er - last - ing Son, Bright-ness of the Fa - ther's glo - ry,
to the hearts of all, In the age - less Word ex - pound-ing

God, the one the right-eous, Lord. In the world's de - spair and
With the Fa - ther ev - er one; Spo - ken by the Word In -
God's own mes-sage for us all. Through the rise and fall of

tur - moil, One firm an - chor holds us fast; God is
car - nate, God of God, be - fore time was; Light of
na - tions One sure faith yet stand - ing fast; God a -

king, his throne e - ter - nal; God the first, and God the last.
Light, to earth de - scend-ing, He re - veals our God to us.
bides, his Word un - chang-ing; God the first, and God the last.

Text: George Briggs, 1875-1959, alt., © 1953, renewed 1981, The Hymn Society. Administered by Hope Publishing Co.
Tune: RUSTINGTON, 8 7 8 7 D; Charles H. Parry, 1848-1918

Spirit of Jesus, If I Love My Neighbor 32

unison

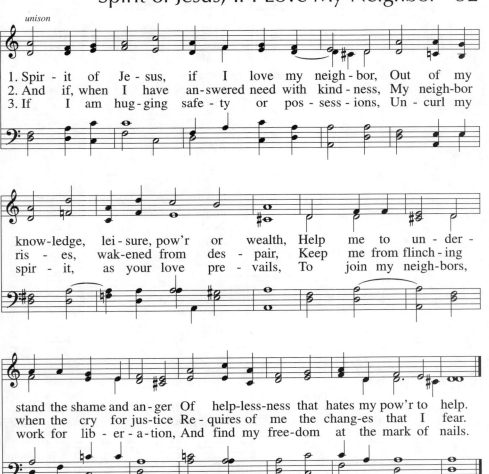

1. Spir - it of Je - sus, if I love my neigh - bor, Out of my
2. And if, when I have an-swered need with kind - ness, My neigh-bor
3. If I am hug - ging safe - ty or pos - sess - ions, Un - curl my

know-ledge, lei - sure, pow'r or wealth, Help me to un - der -
ris - es, wak-ened from des - pair, Keep me from flinch - ing
spir - it, as your love pre - vails, To join my neigh-bors,

stand the shame and an - ger Of help-less-ness that hates my pow'r to help.
when the cry for jus-tice Re - quires of me the chang-es that I fear.
work for lib - er - a-tion, And find my free-dom at the mark of nails.

Text: Brian Wren, © 1975, rev. 1994 by Hope Publishing Co.
Tune: DONNE SECOURS, 11 10 11 10; *Genevan Psalter*, 1551; harm. by Claude Goudimel

33 O Christ, the Healer, We Have Come

1. O Christ, the Heal - er, we have come To pray for health, to plead for friends. How can we fail to be re - stored, When reached by love that nev - er ends?

2. From ev - 'ry ail - ment flesh en - dures Our bod - ies clam - or to be freed; Yet in our hearts we would con - fess That whole - ness is our deep - est need.

3. How strong, O Lord, are our de - sires, How weak our knowl - edge of our - selves! Re - lease in us those heal - ing truths Un - con - scious pride re - sists or shelves.

4. In con - flicts that de - stroy our health We di - ag - nose the world's dis - ease; Our com - mon life de - clares our ills: Is there no cure, O Christ, for these?

5. Grant that we all, made one in faith, In your com - mu - ni - ty may find The whole - ness that, en - rich - ing us, Shall reach the whole of hu - man - kind.

*May be sung in canon.

Text: Fred Pratt Green, 1903-2000, © 1969, Hope Publishing Co.
Tune: TALLIS' CANON, LM; Thomas Tallis, c.1505-1585

unison

1. For all the world Christ died to pur - chase par - don,
2. With all the world the church must share Christ's mes - sage,
3. In all our world, wher - ev - er God may place us,
4. In all our world— in fac - t'ry, shop or school - room,
5. Lord, make us strong to live your gos - pel's full - ness,

For all the world, ex - alt - ed now, he prays;
His word of light, for - give - ness, free - dom, grace:
At home, a - broad, in far - thest parts of earth,
In kitch - en, board - room, mar - ket, of - fice, mill,
Through sin's long strife, for Christ to take our place,

His ris - en life a - vails for all earth's peo - ple—
Not ours a - lone the glad re - lease he of - fers—
Our high - est joy must be to serve our Sav - ior,
We each must make our wit - ness known with bold - ness—
Till all your world shall bow as one be - fore you,

How few yet know his word and walk his ways!
His love em - brac - es all his hu - man race.
And all we are must speak his pow'r and worth.
God's Spir - it works through mor - tal mind and will.
To see, a - dore, and serve you face to face!

Text: Margaret Clarkson, b.1915, © 1987, Hope Publishing Co.
Tune: DONNE SECOURS, 11 10 11 10; *Genevan Psalter*, 1551; harm. by Claude Goudimel

35   You Walk Along Our Shoreline

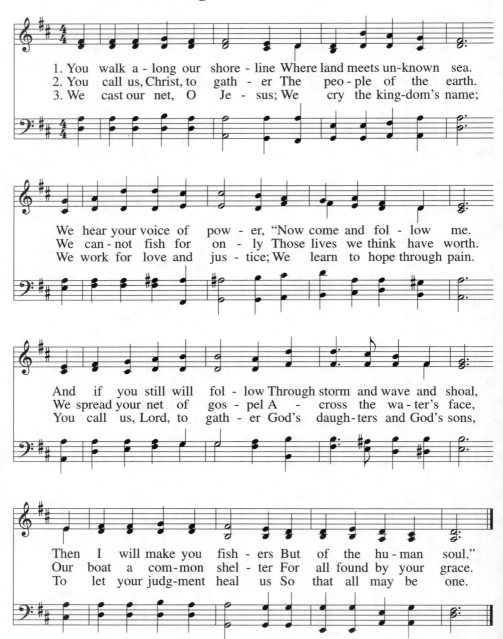

1. You walk a-long our shore-line Where land meets un-known sea.
2. You call us, Christ, to gath-er The peo-ple of the earth.
3. We cast our net, O Je - sus; We cry the king-dom's name;

We hear your voice of pow-er, "Now come and fol-low me.
We can-not fish for on - ly Those lives we think have worth.
We work for love and jus - tice; We learn to hope through pain.

And if you still will fol-low Through storm and wave and shoal,
We spread your net of gos - pel A - cross the wa-ter's face,
You call us, Lord, to gath-er God's daugh-ters and God's sons,

Then I will make you fish - ers But of the hu-man soul."
Our boat a com-mon shel - ter For all found by your grace.
To let your judg-ment heal us So that all may be one.

Text: Sylvia Dunstan, 1955-1993, © 1991, GIA Publications, Inc.
Tune: AURELIA, 7 6 7 6 D; Samuel Sebastian Wesley, 1810-1876

1. Seek for the king-dom with all of your pow'rs!
2. More than the beau-ty that bright-ens the field,
3. Seek then the king-dom dis-cern-ing its signs:
4. Seek for the king-dom with bod-y and mind.

Live by your faith, not the fear in your bone.
More than the wings that are flash-ing in flight,
Peace that de-fus-es the weap-ons of death,
Seek it by ac-tion and stren-u-ous thought.

Think on the ra-ven, con-sid-er the flow'rs:
Je-sus in dy-ing and ris-ing re-vealed
Jus-tice de-feat-ing op-pres-sion's de-signs,
Seek, and in seek-ing by grace you will find

1.- 3. / *4.*

All that is liv-ing is cher-ished and known.
We are en-com-passed by love and by light.
Heal-ing that strength-ens our pulse and our breath.
Won-ders sur-pas-sing the won-ders you sought.

Text: Thomas H. Troeger, b.1945, © 1994, Oxford University Press, Inc.
Tune: OLDHAM, 10 10 10 10; Ron Klusmeier, © 1974

37 Said Judas to Mary

1. Said Ju - das to Mar - y, "Now what will you do With your
2. "Oh Mar - y, O Mar - y, O think of the poor. This
3. "To - mor - row, to - mor - row, I'll think of the poor; To -
4. Said Je - sus to Mar - y, "Your love is so deep To -
5. "The poor of the world are my bo - dy," he said, "To the
6. "My bo - dy will hang on the cross of the world To -

oint - ment so rich and so rare?" "I'll
oint - ment, it could have been sold: And
mor - row," she said, "not to - day; For
day, you may do as you will. To -
end of the world they shall be. The
mor - row," he said, "not to - day. And

pour it all o - ver the feet of the Lord, And I'll
think of the blan - kets and think of the bread You could
dear - er than all of the poor in the world Is my
mor - row, you say, I am go - ing a - way, But my
bread and the blank - ets you give to the poor You'll
Mar - tha and Mar - y will find me a - gain And

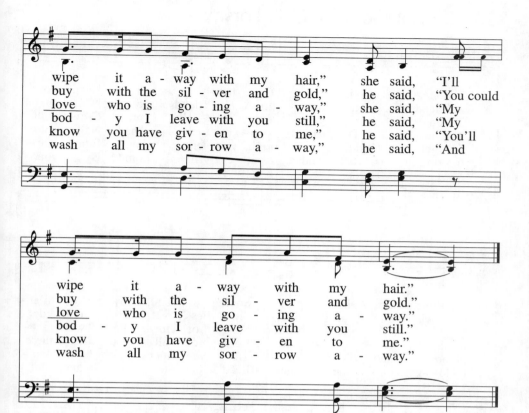

Text: Sydney Carter, b.1915
Tune: JUDAS AND MARY, Irregular; Sydney Carter, b.1915
© 1964, Stainer & Bell Ltd. Administered by Hope Publishing Co.

38 Son of God, by God Forsaken

1. Son of God, by God for-sak-en, Hear your peo-ple's hum-ble plea: Source of Life, by death o'er-tak-en, Feed us from the bar-ren tree.

2. Friend of sin-ners, none be-friends you, Left to die while all de-ride; Sin-less, yet not one de-fends you When con-demned and cru-ci-fied.

3. Son of Man, your foes as-sail you, Crown with cru-el thorns your brow. King of kings, no sword a-vails you In your hour of deep-est woe.

4. Heal-er of the bro-ken, an-guished, Nails your hands and feet im-pale. Lord of all, you hang there van-quished By the death your friends be-wail.

5. Light of light, no bright-ness cheer-ing Rends the gloom of that dread day Till your mer-cy's beams, ap-pear-ing, Drive the clouds of sin a-way.

6. Come, O Christ, and grant us free-dom By your bond-age on the tree. Lead our steps to that fair king-dom Where you reign e-ter-nal-ly.

Text: Herman G. Stuempfle, b.1923, © 1993, GIA Publications, Inc.
Tune: OMNI DIE, 8 7 8 7; Corner's *Cross Catholisch Gesangbuch*, 1631; arr. William Smith Rockstro, 1895

1. "Pre - pare a room for me, Your
2. "This room we have pre - pared; The
3. "Where e - ven two or three Have
4. "Lord Christ, we seek the food Your
5. "My prom - ise I will keep; Your
6. "All thanks and praise to you, Our

Sav - ior, Host and Priest, Where I may gath - er
Ta - ble now is set. We wait your prom - ised
come the Meal to share, Un - seen, but liv - ing,
grace a - lone can give. We come with emp - ty,
hun - ger will be fed, For in this Meal I
Sav - ior, Lord, and Friend, That through this Loaf and

you, my friends, To cel - e - brate the feast."
pres - ence, Lord, Where we once more are met."
lov - ing still, I sure - ly will be there!"
hun - g'ring hearts That we may eat and live."
of - fer you My - self, the liv - ing Bread!"
Cup you share Your love that has no end!"

Text: Herman G. Stuempfle, b.1923, © 2000, GIA Publications, Inc.
Tune: SOUTHWELL, SM; Daman's *Psalmes*, alt.

40   In the Bulb There Is a Flower

1. In the bulb there is a flow - er; In the
2. There's a song in ev - 'ry si - lence, Seek-ing
3. In our end is our be - gin - ning; In our

seed, an ap-ple tree; In co-coons, a hid-den
word and mel-o - dy; There's a dawn in ev - 'ry
time, in - fin - i - ty; In our doubt there is be -

prom - ise: But - ter - flies will soon be free! In the
dark - ness, Bring-ing hope to you and me. From the
liev - ing; In our life, e - ter - ni - ty. In our

cold and snow of win - ter There's a spring that waits to be,
past will come the fu - ture; What it holds, a mys-ter - y,
death, a res - ur - rec - tion; At the last, a vic - to - ry,

Un-re-vealed un-til its sea-son, Some-thing God a-lone can see.

Text: Natalie Sleeth, 1930-1992
Tune: PROMISE, 8 7 8 7 D; Natalie Sleeth, 1930-1992
© 1986, Hope Publishing Co.

Deliver Us, O Lord of Truth   41

1. De - liv - er us, O Lord of Truth, From
2. For you have taught that weight - less words Are
3. When we with bold, fa - mil - iar phrase Con -
4. Lord, help us build on sol - id rock No

speech un - backed by deed, From lives that by their
like the shift - ing sand. When storm and flood come
fess that you are Lord, You ask for lives whose
floods can un - der - mine. May ac - tions fol - low

faith - less - ness De - ny our spo - ken creed.
rag - ing in, They give no place to stand.
faith - ful - ness Sup - ports our spo - ken word.
words we speak; Let creed with deed com - bine.

Text: Herman G. Stuempfle, b.1923, © 1997, GIA Publications, Inc.
Tune: LAND OF REST, CM; American; harm. by Annabel M. Buchanan, 1888-1983, © 1938, J. Fisher and Bro.

42 Within the Father's House

1. With - in the Fa - ther's house The Son has found his home, And to his tem - ple sud - den - ly The Lord of life has come.
2. The doc - tors of the law Gaze on the won-drous child And mar - vel at his gra - cious words Of wis - dom un - de - filed.
3. Yet not to them is giv'n The might - y truth to know, To lift the earth - ly veil which hides In - car - nate God be - low.
4. The se - cret of the Lord Es - capes each hu - man eye, And faith - ful pon-d'ring hearts a - wait The full e - piph - a - ny.
5. Lord, en - ter now our souls And teach us by your grace Each dim re - veal - ing of your - self With lov - ing awe to trace,
6. Till we be - hold your face And know as we are known You, Ho - ly Spir - it, Fa - ther, Son, Co - e - qual Three in One.

Text: James R. Woodford, 1820-1885, alt.
Tune: FRANCONIA, SM; Johann b. Konig, 1691-1758; adapt. by William H. Havergal

unison

1. God's word through-out the ag - es Has
2. The house was full of sad - ness; A
3. He plead - ed for his daugh - ter Be -
4. The house was full of mourn - ers, The
5. He touched her with his speak - ing And
6. He gave the mourn - ers laugh - ter; The
7. Your church is like a daugh - ter Who

been the source of life, And still it rais - es
lit - tle girl had died. Her fa - ther ran to
fore the Son of man: Lord, lay your hand up -
street was dark with gloom, When Je - sus came and
took her by the hand; He gave the girl her
girl an - oth - er chance. He stopped the sad pro -
o - ver-sleeps in death; Lord, touch her with your

peo - ple Out of their tomb of grief.
Je - sus And like a man he cried.
on her And she will live a - gain.
en - tered The still - ness of her room.
Eas - ter And helped her live and stand.
ces - sion By lead - ing death a dance.
Spir - it And bring her back to life.

Text: Dr. Willem Barnard, tr. by Fred Kaan, © 1968, Hope Publishing Co.
Tune: DE EERSTEN ZIJN DE LAATSTEN, 7 6 7 6; Fritz Mehrtens, 1922-1975, © 1973, Interkerkelijke Stichting voor het Kerkenlied

44 On Emmaus' Journey

1. Who are you who walk in sor - row Down Em - ma - us'
2. Who is this who joins our jour - ney, Walk - ing with us
3. Who are you? Our hearts are o - pened In the break - ing
4. Who are we who trav - el with you On our way through
5. "Al - le - lu - ia! Al - le - lu - ia!" Is the Eas - ter

bar - ren road, Hearts dis - traught and hope de - feat - ed,
stride by stride? Un - known Strang - er, can you fath - om
of the bread— Christ the vic - tim, now the vic - tor
life to death? Wom - en, men, the young, the ag - ing,
hymn we sing! Take our life, our joy, our wor - ship

Bent be - neath grief's crush - ing load? Name - less mourn - ers,
Depths of grief for one who died? Then the won - der!
Liv - ing, ris - en from the dead! Great Com - pan - ion
Wak - ened by the Spir - it's breath! At the font you
As the gift of love we bring. You have formed us

we will join you, We who al - so mourn our dead.
When we told you How our dreams to dust have turned,
on our jour - ney, Still sur - prise us with your grace!
claim and name us, Born of wa - ter and the Word.
all one peo - ple Called from ev - 'ry land and race.

We have stood by graves un - yield - ing,
Then you o - pened wide the Scrip - tures
Make each day a new Em - ma - us;
At the ta - ble still you feed us,
Make your church your ser - vant Bod - y,

Eat - en death's bare, bit - ter bread.
Till our hearts with - in us burned!
On our hearts your im - age trace!
Host us as our Ris - en Lord!
Sent to share your heal - ing grace!

Text: Herman G. Stuempfle, b.1923, © 2000, National Association of Pastoral Musicians, admin. by GIA Publications, Inc.
Tune: HOLY MANNA, 8 7 8 7 D; William Moore

45 For Your Gift of God the Spirit

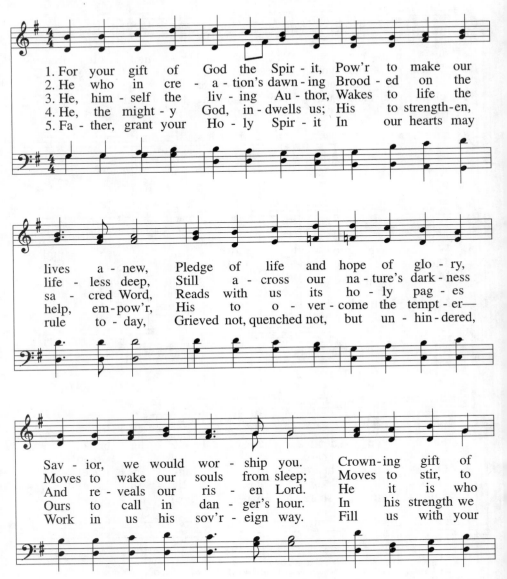

1. For your gift of God the Spir - it, Pow'r to make our
2. He who in cre - a - tion's dawn - ing Brood - ed on the
3. He, him - self the liv - ing Au - thor, Wakes to life the
4. He, the might - y God, in - dwells us; His to strength-en,
5. Fa - ther, grant your Ho - ly Spir - it In our hearts may

lives a - new, Pledge of life and hope of glo - ry,
life - less deep, Still a - cross our na - ture's dark - ness
sa - cred Word, Reads with us its ho - ly pag - es
help, em - pow'r, His to o - ver - come the tempt - er—
rule to - day, Grieved not, quenched not, but un - hin - dered,

Sav - ior, we would wor - ship you. Crown-ing gift of
Moves to wake our souls from sleep; Moves to stir, to
And re - veals our ris - en Lord. He it is who
Ours to call in dan - ger's hour. In his strength we
Work in us his sov'r - eign way. Fill us with your

res - ur - rec - tion, Sent from your as - cend - ed throne;
draw, to quick - en, Thrusts us through with sense of sin;
works with - in us Teach - ing reb - el hearts to pray,
dare to bat - tle All the rag - ing hosts of sin,
ho - ly ful - ness, God the Fa - ther, Spir - it, Son;

Ful - ness of the ver - y God - head
Brings to birth and seals and fills us—
He whose ho - ly in - ter - ces - sions
And by him a - lone we con - quer
In us, through us, then, for - ev - er

Come to make your life our own.
Sav - ing Ad - vo - cate with - in.
Rise for us both night and day.
Foes with - out and foes with - in.
Shall your per - fect will be done.

Text: Margaret Clarkson, © 1960, 1976, renewed 1988 by Hope Publishing Co.
Tune: HYMN TO JOY, 8 7 8 7 D; arr. from Ludwig van Beethoven, 1770-1827, by Edward Hodges, 1796-1867.

46 Here From All Nations

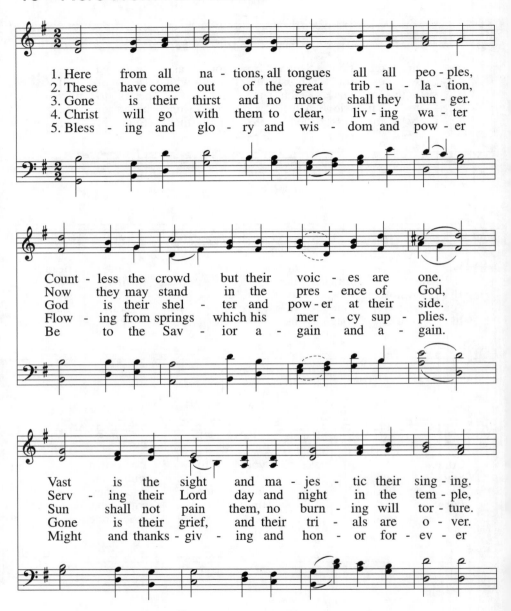

1. Here from all na - tions, all tongues all all peo - ples,
2. These have come out of the great trib - u - la - tion,
3. Gone is their thirst and no more shall they hun - ger.
4. Christ will go with them to clear, liv - ing wa - ter
5. Bless - ing and glo - ry and wis - dom and pow - er

Count - less the crowd but their voic - es are one.
Now they may stand in the pres - ence of God,
God is their shel - ter and pow - er at their side.
Flow - ing from springs which his mer - cy sup - plies.
Be to the Sav - ior a - gain and a - gain.

Vast is the sight and ma - jes - tic their sing - ing.
Serv - ing their Lord day and night in the tem - ple,
Sun shall not pain them, no burn - ing will tor - ture.
Gone is their grief, and their tri - als are o - ver.
Might and thanks - giv - ing and hon - or for - ev - er

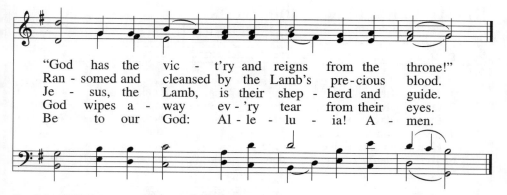

"God has the vic - t'ry and reigns from the throne!"
Ran - somed and cleansed by the Lamb's pre - cious blood.
Je - sus, the Lamb, is their shep - herd and guide.
God wipes a - way ev - 'ry tear from their eyes.
Be to our God: Al - le - lu - ia! A - men.

Text: Christopher Idle, © 1973, Jubilate Hymns Ltd. Administered by Hope Publishing Co.
Tune: O QUANTA QUALIA, 11 10 11 10; *Paris Antiphoner*, 1681; adapt. by Francois de la Feillée; harm. by David Evans, 1874-1948, © Oxford University Press, Inc.

Crashing Waters at Creation 47

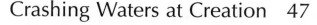

1. Crash - ing wa - ters at cre - a - tion,
2. Part - ing wa - ter stood and trem - bled
3. Cleans - ing wa - ter once at Jor - dan
4. Liv - ing wa - ter, nev - er end - ing,

Or - dered by the Spir - it's breath, First to wit - ness
As the cap - tives passed on through, Wash - ing off the
Closed a - round the one fore - told, O - pened to re -
Quench the thirst and flood the soul. Well - spring, Source of

day's be - gin - ning From the bright - ness of night's death.
chains of bond - age— Chan - nel to a life made new.
veal the glo - ry Ev - er new and ev - er old.
life e - ter - nal, Drench our dry - ness, make us whole.

Text: Sylvia Dunstan, 1955-1993, © 1991, GIA Publications, Inc.
Tune: STUTTGART, 8 7 8 7; *Psalmodia Sacra*, 1715; adapt. and harm. by William Henry Havergal, 1793-1870, alt.

48 The First Day of the Week

1. The first day of the week His
2. O - be - dient to his word, They
3. Each day through - out the week As
4. So on this joy - ful day From
5. How soon we forge a - gain The
6. To - day his peo - ple meet, To -

own, in sad de - spair, Could not be - lieve for
shared what Je - sus gave, And, one in him, in
on the Lord's own day, They walked in new - found
need - less bur - dens freed, We keep the feast he
fet - ters of our past: As long as Je - sus
day his word is sown; Lord Je - sus, show us

ver - y joy The ris - en Lord was there.
break - ing bread Knew what it cost to save.
lib - er - ty His true and liv - ing way.
made for us To fit our in - most need.
lives in us So long our free - doms last.
how to use This day we call your own.

Text: Fred Pratt Green, 1903-2000, © 1969, Hope Publishing Co.
Tune: ST. THOMAS, SM; Aaron Williams; harm. by Lowell Mason, 1792-1872

It Shocked Them that the Master Did Not Fast 49

1. It shocked them that the Master did not fast;
2. How short a time for such fes - tiv - i - ty!
3. Fast - ing and feast - ing, there is room for each;

But Je - sus wit - ti - ly de - fends
Soon they must mourn a Bride - groom slain,
But, Lord, let not our fast - ing strip

A way of life less stern than John's:
And, fast - ing, share his suf - fer - ing.
Our souls of joy, or feast - ing blunt

Fast - ing would ill be - come the Bride - groom's friends.
Then, one mo - men - tous morn - ing, feast a - gain!
The dis - ci - plines of our dis - ci - ple - ship.

Text: Fred Pratt Green, 1903-2000, © 1982, Hope Publishing Co.
Tune: MINTWOOD, 10 8 8 10; James J. Chepponis, b.1956, © 1986, GIA Publications, Inc.

50　A Year of God's Favor

1. A year of God's favor Christ prom-ised, and more:
2. This word is ful-filled in be-liev-ers to-day,
3. Ful-filled in our liv-ing be God's word to-day,

Good news to the pris-'ner, the weak and the poor,
In wom-en and men who would fol-low Christ's way.
Ful-filled in our lov-ing, our work and our play,

Re-cov-'ry of sense to the deaf and the blind,
Re-spond, then, with glad-ness, in all that you do:
Ful-filled now in jus-tice, in mer-cy and peace,

Full heal-ing for spir-it, for bod-y and mind.
A life-time of fa-vor is of-fered to you!
In joy-ful thanks-giv-ing and praise with-out cease.

Text: Delores Dufner, OSB, © 1995, Sisters of St. Benedict
Tune: ST. DENIO, 11 11 11 11; Robert's *Canaidau y Cyssegr*, 1839

1. Come, join in Ca - na's feast Where Christ is hon - ored guest. He wel - comes all who come to taste The wine his hands have blessed.
2. The old wine now is gone From jars that stand a - part. No long - er can it sat - is - fy The yearn - ing, thirst - ing heart.
3. But Christ, the Word made flesh, Bids wa - ter turn to wine. He fills our emp - ty cups a - gain With grace and truth di - vine.
4. Come, friends, and share the feast; Here drink the wine sup - plied By him who is both guest and host; For us, the cru - ci - fied.
5. For now he lives and reigns Through all e - ter - ni - ty With Fa - ther, Spir - it, three in one, The glo - rious Trin - i - ty.

Text: Herman G. Stuempfle, b.1923, © 1993, GIA Publications, Inc.
Tune: ST. THOMAS, SM; Aaron Williams; harm. by Lowell Mason, 1792-1872

52 When Jesus Passed through Jericho

1. When Je - sus passed through Jer - i - cho, The
2. Zac - chae - us, small and scorned by all, Thought
3. He watched be - neath the sway - ing boughs The
4. Zac - chae - us took the Lord straight home And,
5. The friend of sin - ners Je - sus was And
6. In - stead, when bowed by guilt or grief We

peo - ple crowd - ed round To see the one who
he should al - so see The Mas - ter when he
man from Gal - i - lee. And Je - sus saw his
while they shared a meal, Told Je - sus he would
is the same to - day. He nev - er sees a
seek the Lord to see, He sets be - fore us

healed the sick, By whom the lost were
came to town, And so he climbed a
lone - ly face And said, "Come, eat with
help the poor And nev - er cheat or
lone - ly face And looks the oth - er
bread and wine And says, "Come, eat with

found, By whom the lost were found.
tree, And so he climbed a tree.
me." And said, "Come, eat with me."
steal, And nev - er cheat or steal.
way, And looks the oth - er way.
me." And says, "Come, eat with me."

Text: Herman G. Stuempfle, b.1923, © 1993, GIA Publications, Inc.
Tune: DOVE OF PEACE, 8 6 8 66; American Folk Melody; harm. by Charles H. Webb, © 1989, United Methodist Publishing House

Come to Me, O Weary Traveler 53

1. Come to Me, O wea - ry trav - 'ler;
2. Do not fear, my yoke is eas - y;
3. Take my yoke and leave your trou - bles;
4. Rest in Me, O wea - ry trav - 'ler;

Come to Me with your dis - tress; Come to Me, you
Do not fear, my bur - den's light; Do not fear the
Take my yoke and come with me. Take my yoke, I
Rest in Me and do not fear. Rest in Me, my

heav - y bur - dened; Come to Me and find your rest.
path be - fore you; Do not run from Me in fright.
am be - side you; Take and learn hu - mil - i - ty.
heart is gen - tle; Rest and cast a - way your care.

Text: Sylvia Dunstan, 1955-1993, © 1991, GIA Publications, Inc.
Tune: STUTTGART, 8 7 8 7; *Psalmodia Sacra*, 1715; adapt. and harm. by William Henry Havergal, 1793-1870, alt.

54 From the River to the Desert

unison

1. From the riv - er to the des - ert,
2. If you are the one God choos - es,
3. If you are the one God of - fers,
4. If you are the one God prom - ised,
5. Since we are the ones you gath - er,

For - ty days that give no rest;
You can turn these stones to bread.
Leap in - to the an - gels' hands.
You could still bow down to me.
And from sin and death have freed,

Fast and pray and wait and wres - tle,
See, the chil - dren yearn and hun - ger,
Show your pow - er and your glo - ry,
Look at all the wealth of na - tions,
Je - sus, know - ing all our weak - ness,

Face the Ad - ver - sar - y's test:
By your deeds the poor are fed.
Then be - lief will sweep the land.
I will give you all you see.
Now at God's high al - tar plead.

Prince of Peace and Prince of Dark - ness
"Don't you know that it is writ - ten:
"Don't you know that it is writ - ten:
"Don't you know that it is writ - ten:
For we know that it is writ - ten

Meet in lone - ly wil - der - ness.
No one lives by bread a - lone."
Do not tempt the Lord your God."
Wor - ship God and God a - lone."
That your grace is all we need.

Text: Sylvia Dunstan, 1955-1993, © 1991, GIA Publications, Inc.
Tune: PICARDY, 8 7 8 7 8 7; French Carol; harm. by Richard Proulx, b.1937, © 1986, GIA Publications, Inc.

55   O Christ, Who Called the Twelve

1. O Christ, who called the Twelve To rise and fol-low you, For-sak-ing old, fa-mil-iar ways For ven-tures bold and new: Grant us to hear your

2. O Christ, who taught the Twelve The truth for a-ges sealed, Whose words and works a-wak-ened faith, The ways of God re-vealed: In-struct us now, we

3. O Christ, who led the Twelve A-mong the des-o-late And broke as bread of life for all Your love com-pas-sion-ate: Lead us a-long the

4. O Christ, who sent the Twelve On roads they'd nev-er trod To serve, to suf-fer, teach, pro-claim The near-er reign of God: Send us on ways where

5. O Christ, th'a-pos-tles' Lord, The mar-tyrs' strength and song, The cru-ci-fied and ris-en king To whom the saints be-long: Though gen-er-a-tions

call To risk se - cu - ri - ty And,
pray, By your em - pow'r - ing Word. True
ways Where hope has near - ly died And
faith Tran - scends ti - mid - i - ty, Where
pass, Our tri - bute still we bring, Our

bound in heart and will to you, Find per - fect lib - er - ty.
teach - er, be for all who seek Their light, their life, their Lord.
help us climb the lone - ly hills Where love is cru - ci - fied.
love in-forms and hope sus-tains Both life and min - is - try.
hymns a sac - ri - fice of praise, Our lives an of - fer - ing.

Text: Herman G. Stuempfle, b.1923, © 1993, GIA Publications, Inc.
Tune: TERRA BEATA, SMD; English; adapt. by Franklin L. Sheppard, 1915

56 Like the Murmur of the Dove's Song

unison

1. Like the mur - mur of the dove's song, Like the chal - lenge of her flight, Like the vig - or of the wind's rush, Like the new flame's ea - ger might: Come, Ho - ly Spir - it, come.

2. To the mem - bers of Christ's bod - y, To the branch-es of the vine, To the church in faith as - sem - bled, To her midst as gift and sign: Come, Ho - ly Spir - it, come.

3. With the heal - ing of di - vi - sion, With the cease - less voice of prayer, With the pow'r to love and wit - ness, With the peace be - yond com - pare: Come, Ho - ly Spir - it, come.

Text: Carl P. Daw, Jr., b.1944, © 1982, Hope Publishing Co.
Tune: BRIDEGROOM, 8 7 8 7 6; Peter Cutts, b.1937, © 1969, Hope Publishing Co.

1. A blind man sat beside the road And begged for char - i - ty Un - til he heard a stran - ger's step And asked, "Who can this be?"

2. "Who can this be, and will he stop For one as poor as I?" Then voic - es pierced his dark - ness deep: "The Lord is pass - ing by."

3. "He must not pass me by," he cried; "He must in pit - y see These emp - ty hands, these sight - less eyes! Have mer - cy, Lord, on me!"

4. Then Je - sus stopped, in mer - cy spoke; Those sight - less eyes he healed Which, o - pened wide, by faith made whole, The Son of God re - vealed.

5. Our blind - ness cries for vi - sion bright, Our pov - er - ty for grace. O Lord, have mer - cy now on us; To us re - veal your face.

Text: Herman G. Stuempfle, b.1923, © 1993, GIA Publications, Inc.
Tune: NEW BRITAIN, CM; *Virginia Harmony*, 1831; harm. by Edwin O. Excell, 1851-1921

58 The Call Is Clear and Simple

1. The call is clear and sim - ple: "Love God and hu - man -
2. God, help us sort our mo - tives, That lov - ing may be
3. God, teach us strength and wis - dom When false love takes the
4. O wise and ho - ly Lov - er, Teach us as sea - sons

kind," But love de - mands much wis - dom And
whole. High aims or base am - bi - tion? Com -
lead. Too well we learn sub - mis - sion And
turn To know our - selves and oth - ers— Deep,

clar - i - ty of mind. "Be wi - ly as a
pas - sion or con - trol? Then help us clear our
si - lence our own need. When oth - ers would mis -
hon - est love to learn. So may we nur - ture

ser - pent, Though gen - tle as a dove," For
sched - ules Of ev - 'ry fran - tic task That
use us Or lure us t'ward the wrong, God,
liv - ing In all we say and do, In

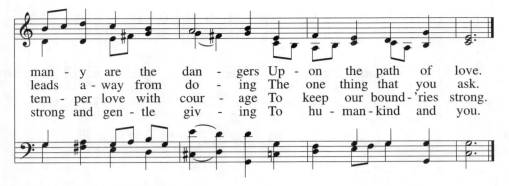

man - y are the dan - gers Up - on the path of love.
leads a - way from do - ing The one thing that you ask.
tem - per love with cour - age To keep our bound - 'ries strong.
strong and gen - tle giv - ing To hu - man - kind and you.

Text: Ruth Duck, b.1947, © 1992, GIA Publications, Inc.
Tune: PASSION CHORALE, 7 6 7 6 D; Hans Leo Hassler, 1564-1612; harm. by J. S. Bach, 1685-1750

How Great Your Mercy, Risen Lord 59

1. How great your mer - cy, ris - en Lord, That
2. But did not hands that once took bread The
3. Lord, guard the hands we now ex - tend From
4. Then teach us how to pray with you, "Your

you with us should dine, That you should place with -
sil - ver coins then seize, And was not friend - ship's
sin's de - fil - ing stain And bind the lives which
will, not mine, O God!" And when you call, Lord,

in our hands Your gifts of bread and wine!
bond be - trayed Be - neath the ol - ive trees?
now you bless In love's en - cir - cling chain.
help us walk The path of pain you trod.

Text: Herman G. Stuempfle, b.1923, © 1997, GIA Publications, Inc.
Tune: ST. PETER, CM; Alexander Robert Reinagle

60 How Clear Is Our Vocation, Lord

1. How clear is our vo - ca - tion, Lord, When
2. But if, for - get - ful, we should find Your
3. We mar - vel how your saints be - come In
4. In what you give us, Lord, to do, To -

once we heed your call: To live ac - cord - ing
yoke is hard to bear; If world - ly pres - sures
hin - dranc - es more sure; Whose joy - ful vir - tues
geth - er or a - lone, In old rou - tines and

to your word, And dai - ly learn, re -
fray the mind, And love it - self can -
put to shame The cas - ual way we
ven - tures new, May we not cease to

freshed, re - stored, That you are Lord of
not un - wind Its tan - gled skein of
wear your name, And by our faults ob -
look to you, The cross you hung up -

all.   And will not let us fall.
care: Our in - ward life re - pair.
scure   Your pow'r to cleanse and cure.
on—   All you en - deav - ored done.

Text: Fred Pratt Green, 1903-2000, © 1982, Hope Publishing Co.
Tune: REPTON, 8 6 8 8 66; C. Hubert H. Parry, 1848-1918

If All You Want, Lord, Is My Heart   61

1. If all you want, Lord, is my heart, My
2. If all you want, Lord, is my mind, My
3. If heart and mind would both suf - fice, While
4. But since, O God, you want them all To

heart is yours a - lone— Pro - vid - ing I may
mind be - longs to you, But let my heart re -
I kept strength and soul, At least I would not
shape with your own hand, I pray for grace to

set a - part My mind to be my own.
main in - clined To do what it would do.
sac - ri - fice Com - plete - ly my con - trol.
heed your call To live your first com - mand.

Text: Thomas H. Troeger, b.1945, © 1994, Oxford University Press, Inc.
Tune: MORNING SONG, CM; Wyeth's *Repository of Sacred Music*, 1813; harm. by C. Winfred Douglas, 1867-1944

62 As a Chalice Cast of Gold

1. As a chal-ice cast of gold, Burn-ished, bright and
2. Save me from the sooth-ing sin Of the emp-ty
3. When I bend up-on my knees, Clasp my hands or
4. When I dance or chant your praise, When I sing a

brimmed with wine, Make me, Lord, as fit to hold
cul-tic deed And the pi-ous, bab-bling din
bow my head, Let my spo-ken, pub-lic pleas
song or hymn, When I preach your lov-ing ways,

Grace and truth and love di-vine. Let my praise and
Of the claimed but un-lived creed. Let my ac-tions,
Be dir-ect-ly, sim-ply said, Free of tan-gled
Let my heart add its A-men. Let each cher-ished,

wor-ship start With the cleans-ing of my heart.
Lord, ex-press What my tongue and lips pro-fess.
words that mask What my soul would plain-ly ask.
out-ward rite Thus re-flect your in-ward light.

Text: Thomas H. Troeger, b.1945, © 1994, Oxford University Press, Inc.
Tune: DIX, 7 7 7 7 77; arr. from Conrad Kocher, 1786-1872, by William H. Monk, 1823-1889

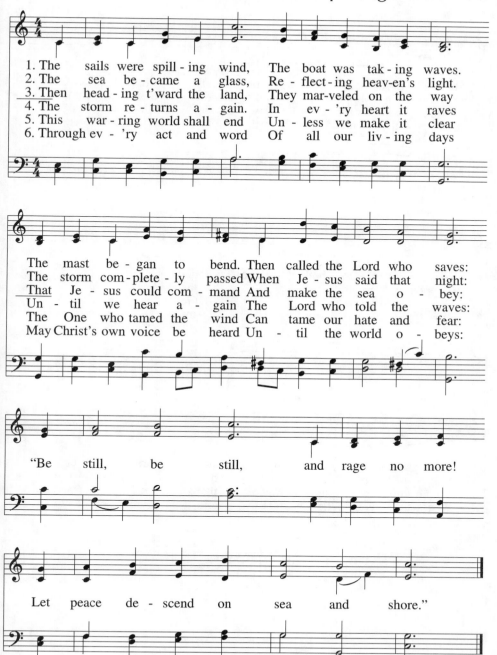

1. The sails were spill-ing wind, The boat was tak-ing waves.
2. The sea be-came a glass, Re-flect-ing heav-en's light.
3. Then head-ing t'ward the land, They mar-veled on the way
4. The storm re-turns a-gain. In ev-'ry heart it raves
5. This war-ring world shall end Un-less we make it clear
6. Through ev-'ry act and word Of all our liv-ing days

The mast be-gan to bend. Then called the Lord who saves:
The storm com-plete-ly passed When Je-sus said that night:
That Je-sus could com-mand And make the sea o-bey:
Un-til we hear a-gain The Lord who told the waves:
The One who tamed the wind Can tame our hate and fear:
May Christ's own voice be heard Un-til the world o-beys:

"Be still, be still, and rage no more!

Let peace de-scend on sea and shore."

Text: Thomas H. Troeger, b.1945, © 1994, Oxford University Press, Inc.
Tune: DARWALL'S 148TH, 6 6 6 6 88; John Darwall, 1731-1789; harm. from *The Hymnal 1940*

64 You, Lord, Are Both Lamb and Shepherd

unison

1. You, Lord, are both Lamb and Shep - herd.
2. Clothed in light up - on the moun - tian,
3. You, who walk each day be - side us,
4. Wor - thy is our earth - ly Je - sus!

You, Lord, are both prince and slave.
Stripped of might up - on the cross,
Sit in pow - er at God's side.
Wor - thy is our cos - mic Christ!

You, peace - mak - er and sword - bring - er
Shin - ing in e - ter - nal glo - ry,
You, who preach a way that's nar - row,
Wor - thy your de - feat and vic - t'ry.

Of the way you took and gave.
Beg - gar'd by a sol - dier's toss,
Have a love that reach - es wide.
Wor - thy still your peace and strife.

You, the ev - er - last - ing in - stant;
You, the ev - er - last - ing in - stant;
You, the ev - er - last - ing in - stant;
You, the ev - er - last - ing in - stant;

You, whom we both scorn and crave.
You, who are our gift and cost.
You, who are our pil - grim guide.
You, who are our death and life.

Text: Sylvia Dunstan, 1955-1993, © 1991, GIA Publications, Inc.
Tune: PICARDY, 8 7 8 7 8 7; French Carol; harm. by Richard Proulx, b.1937, © 1986, GIA Publications, Inc.

65   Jesus, Tempted in the Desert

1. Je - sus, tempt - ed in the des - ert,
2. Je - sus, tempt - ed at the tem - ple,
3. Je - sus, tempt - ed on the moun - tain
4. When we face temp - ta - tion's pow - er,

Lone - ly, hun - gry, filled with dread:
High a - bove its an - cient wall:
By the lure of vast do - main:
Lone - ly, strug - gling, filled with dread,

"Use your pow'r," the tempt - er tells him;
"Throw your - self from loft - y tur - ret;
"Fall be - fore me! Be my ser - vant!
Christ, who knew the tempt - er's ho - ur,

"Turn these bar - ren rocks to bread!"
An - gels wait to break your fall!"
Glo - ry, fame, you're sure to gain!"
Come and be our liv - ing bread.

"Not a - lone by bread," he an - swers,
Je - sus shuns such emp - ty mar - vels,
Je - sus sees the daz - zling vi - sion,
By your grace, pro - tect, pre - serve us

"Can the hu - man heart be filled.
Feats that fick - le crowds re - quest:
Turns his eyes an - oth - er way:
Lest we fall, your trust be - tray.

On - ly by the Word that calls us
"God, whose grace pro - tects, pre - serves us,
"God a - lone de - serves our hom - age!
Yours, a - bove all oth - er voic - es,

Is our deep - est hun - ger stilled!"
We must nev - er vain - ly test."
God a - lone will I o - bey!"
Be the Word we hear, o - bey.

Text: Herman G. Stuempfle, b.1923, © 1993, GIA Publications, Inc.
Tune: EBENEZER, 8 7 8 7 D; Thomas J. Williams, 1869-1944

66 The Ranks of Death with Trophy Grim

1. The ranks of death with tro - phy grim Through an - cient streets once trod And sud - den - ly con - front - ed Christ, The might - y Son of God. A wid - ow's tears e - voked his Word; He

2. The ranks of death and Lord of Life Stood face to face that hour; And Christ took up the an - cient strife With words of awe - some pow'r. "Young man, a - rise!" he or - dered loud, And

3. Death's pow - er holds us still in thrall And bears us t'ward the tomb. Death's dark - 'ning clouds hang like a pall That threat - ens earth with doom. But you have bro - ken death's em - brace And

stopped the bear-ers' tread. "Weep not," in pit - y
death de - feat - ed lay. The wid - ow's son cast
torn a - way its sting. Re - store to life our

spoke the Lord To her whose son was dead.
off his shroud And strode from death a - way.
mor - tal race! Raise us, O ris - en King!

Text: Herman G. Stuempfle, b.1923, © 2000, GIA Publications, Inc.
Tune: KINGSFOLD, CMD; English; harm. by Ralph Vaughan Williams, 1872-1958, © Oxford University Press, Inc.

1. Let us come now to the king - dom
2. Let us come now to the king - dom

Where we're greet - ed by our Lord,
Where all hun - gry souls are fed,

Where our feet are washed in glo - ry
Where our drink is peace and glad - ness

And our en - er - gies re - stored,
And God's right - eous - ness our bread,

Where the saints have come to join us
Where each stran - ger is our neigh - bor

From the west and from the east,
And each neigh - bor next of kin,

Where from north and south they've gath - ered
Where Christ waits for all God's chil - dren,

To help cel - e - brate the feast!
So the ban - quet can be - gin!

Text: Rae E. Whitney, © 1994, Selah Publishing Co., Inc.
Tune: HYFRYDOL, 8 7 8 7 D; Rowland H. Prichard, 1811-1887

68 Shepherd, Do You Tramp the Hills

1. "Shep - herd, do you tramp the hills, Track-ing down one
2. "Wom - an, do you scour the house Just to find one
3. "Fa - ther, does your heart still bleed For a child who
4. Shep - herd, search - er, par - ent's care— By what im - age

stray - ing sheep, Leav - ing nine - ty - nine be - hind
coin that's lost? Since you have the oth - er nine,
chose to roam— Reb - el, row - dy, far a - way,
can we name Spend-thrift love, im - pas-sioned grace,

With no guard the watch to keep?" "But that one I
Is it real - ly worth the cost?" "But that coin you
Spurn - ing love and scorn - ing home?" "But that rest - less,
In - can - des - cent as a flame? Christ, be - yond all

call by name; She will hear and know my voice.
count so small Has for me a spe - cial worth.
reck - less boy Nev - er can my love out - run!
words you spoke, Sto - ries that with won - der glow,

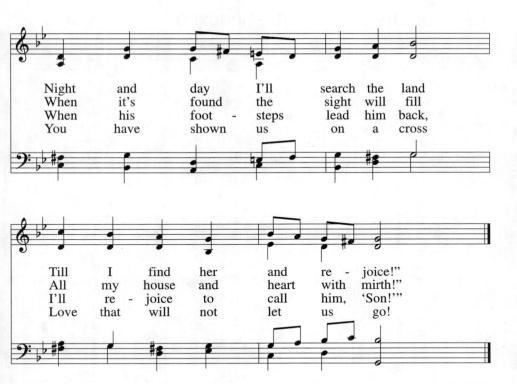

Night and day I'll search the land
When it's found the sight will fill
When his foot - steps lead him back,
You have shown us on a cross

Till I find her and re - joice!"
All my house and heart with mirth!"
I'll re - joice to call him, 'Son!'"
Love that will not let us go!

Text: Herman G. Stuempfle, b.1923, © 2000, GIA Publications, Inc.
Tune: ARFON, 7 7 7 7 D; Welsh Melody

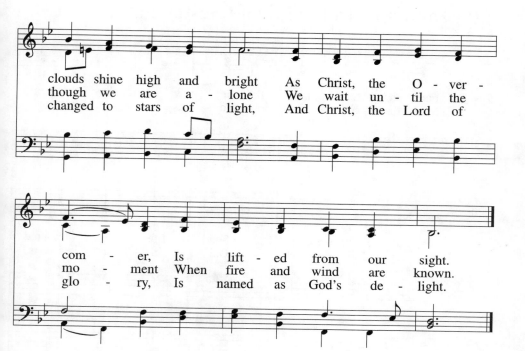

clouds shine high and bright As Christ, the O - ver -
though we are a - lone We wait un - til the
changed to stars of light, And Christ, the Lord of

com - er, Is lift - ed from our sight.
mo - ment When fire and wind are known.
glo - ry, Is named as God's de - light.

Text: Sylvia Dunstan, 1955-1993, © 1995, GIA Publications, Inc.
Tune: ST. THEODULPH, 7 6 7 6 D; Melchior Teschner, 1584-1635

70 Faith and Truth and Life Bestowing

1. Faith and truth and life be-stow-ing, O-pen now the Scrip-tures, Lord, Seed to life e-ter-nal sow-ing Scat-tered on the wind a-broad. Let not hearts, your word re-ceiv-ing, Like a bar-ren field be found, Choked with thorns and

2. May the Spir-it's pow'r un-ceas-ing Bring to life the hid-den grain, Dai-ly in our hearts in-creas-ing, Bear-ing fruit that shall re-main. So in Scrip-ture, song and sto-ry, Sav-ior, may your voice be heard. Till our eyes be-

un - be - liev - ing, Shal-low earth or ston - y ground.
hold your glo - ry Give us ears to hear your word.

Text: Timothy Dudley-Smith, b.1926, © 1997, Hope Publishing Co.
Tune: BEACH SPRING, 8 7 8 7D; attr. Benjamin Franklin White, 1844; harm. by Ronald A. Nelson, © 1978, *Lutheran Book of Worship*

Are You the Coming One   71

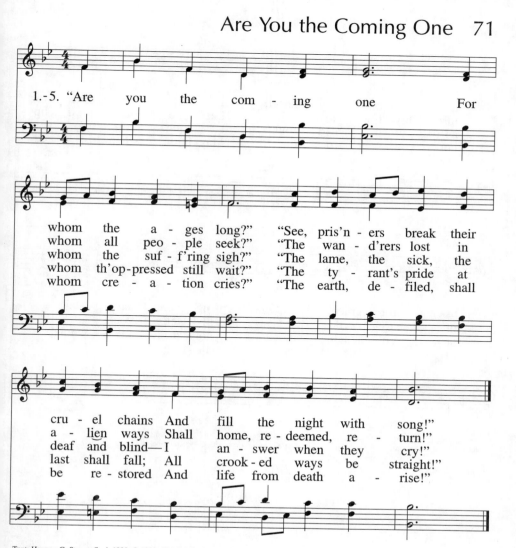

1.-5. "Are you the com - ing one For

whom the a - ges long?" "See, pris'n - ers break their
whom all peo - ple seek?" "The wan - d'rers lost in
whom the suf - f'ring sigh?" "The lame, the sick, the
whom th'op-pressed still wait?" "The ty - rant's pride at
whom cre - a - tion cries?" "The earth, de - filed, shall

cru - el chains And fill the night with song!"
a - lien ways Shall home, re - deemed, re - turn!"
deaf and blind—I an - swer when they cry!"
last shall fall; All crook - ed ways be straight!"
be re - stored And life from death a - rise!"

Text: Herman G. Stuempfle, b.1923, © 1993, GIA Publications, Inc.
Tune: FESTAL SONG, SM; William H. Walter

72 Here, Master, In This Quiet Place

1. Here, Master, in this quiet place, Where
2. If self upon its sick-ness feeds And
3. You nev-er said 'You ask too much' To
4. But if the thing I most de-sire Is

an-y-one may kneel, I al-so come to
turns my life to gall, Let me not brood up-
an-y trou-bled soul. I long to feel your
not your way for me, May faith, when test-ed

ask for grace, Be-liev-ing you can heal.
on my needs, But sim-ply tell you all.
heal-ing touch— Will you not make me whole?
in the fire, Prove its in-teg-ri-ty.

Text: Fred Pratt Green, 1903-2000, © 1974, Hope Publishing Co.
Tune: LAND OF REST, CM; American; harm. by Annabel M. Buchanan, 1888-1983, © 1938, J. Fisher and Bro.

1. Your ways are not our own. O gra-cious God most high, Yet we would fol-low in your paths And on your love re-ly.
2. Christ teach-es us to bless The ones who curse and harm, To turn the oth-er cheek when struck, At-tack-ers to dis-arm.
3. Yet, we can-not ex-cuse A-buse in an-y form, For all are chil-dren of your care, And love must be our norm.
4. How shall we show your love, Your par-don to be-lieve? You bid us share as we are blessed And give as we re-ceive.
5. For-give-ness is our joy, Re-ceiv-ing, giv-ing, too. Keep us from judg-ments hard and cruel, That we may dwell with you.

Text: Lavon Bayler, b.1933, © 1988, The Pilgrim Press
Tune: SWABIA, SM; Johann M. Speiss, 1715-1772; adapt. by William H. Havergal, 1793-1870

74 We Turn our Eyes to Heaven

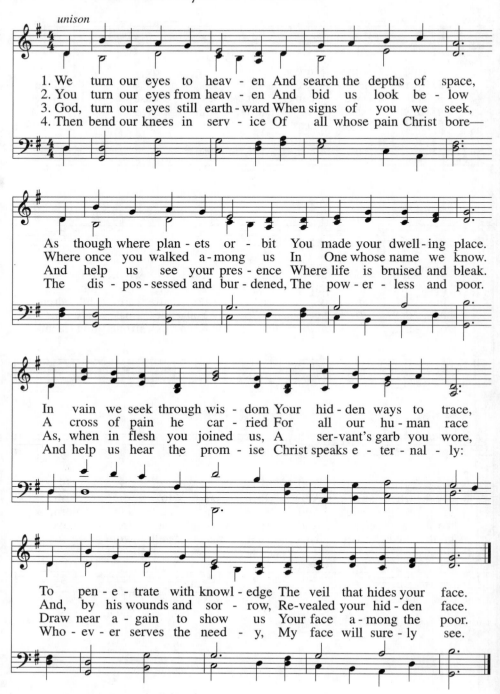

unison

1. We turn our eyes to heav - en And search the depths of space,
2. You turn our eyes from heav - en And bid us look be - low
3. God, turn our eyes still earth - ward When signs of you we seek,
4. Then bend our knees in serv - ice Of all whose pain Christ bore—

As though where plan - ets or - bit You made your dwell - ing place.
Where once you walked a - mong us In One whose name we know.
And help us see your pres - ence Where life is bruised and bleak.
The dis - pos - sessed and bur - dened, The pow - er - less and poor.

In vain we seek through wis - dom Your hid - den ways to trace,
A cross of pain he car - ried For all our hu - man race
As, when in flesh you joined us, A ser - vant's garb you wore,
And help us hear the prom - ise Christ speaks e - ter - nal - ly:

To pen - e - trate with knowl - edge The veil that hides your face.
And, by his wounds and sor - row, Re - vealed your hid - den face.
Draw near a - gain to show us Your face a - mong the poor.
Who - ev - er serves the need - y, My face will sure - ly see.

Text: Herman G. Stuempfle, b.1923, © 1997, GIA Publications, Inc.
Tune: MERLE'S TUNE, 7 6 7 6 D; Hal H. Hopson, b.1933, © 1983, Hope Publishing Co.

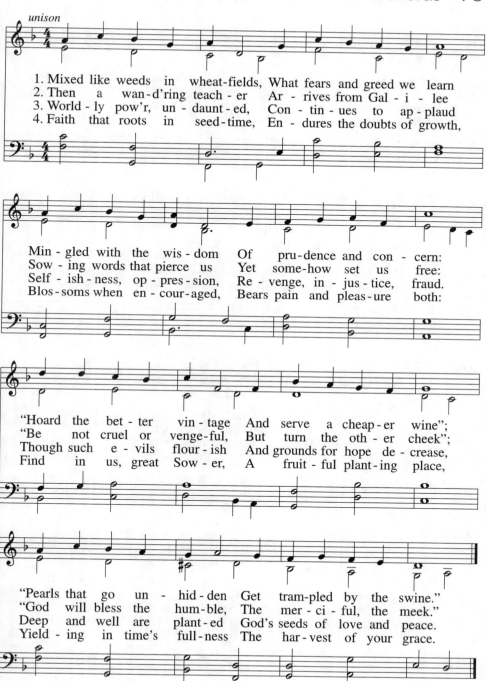

unison

1. Mixed like weeds in wheat-fields, What fears and greed we learn
2. Then a wan-d'ring teach-er Ar - rives from Gal - i - lee
3. World - ly pow'r, un - daunt-ed, Con - tin - ues to ap - plaud
4. Faith that roots in seed-time, En - dures the doubts of growth,

Min - gled with the wis - dom Of pru-dence and con - cern:
Sow - ing words that pierce us Yet some-how set us free:
Self - ish - ness, op - pres - sion, Re - venge, in - jus - tice, fraud.
Blos - soms when en - cour-aged, Bears pain and pleas-ure both:

"Hoard the bet - ter vin - tage And serve a cheap-er wine";
"Be not cruel or venge-ful, But turn the oth - er cheek";
Though such e - vils flour - ish And grounds for hope de - crease,
Find in us, great Sow - er, A fruit - ful plant-ing place,

"Pearls that go un - hid-den Get tram-pled by the swine."
"God will bless the hum-ble, The mer - ci - ful, the meek."
Deep and well are plant-ed God's seeds of love and peace.
Yield - ing in time's full-ness The har - vest of your grace.

Text: Carl P. Daw, Jr., b.1944
Tune: DARNEL, 6 6 6 6 D; Carl P. Daw, Jr., b.1944

1. Re - joice, O Zi - on's daugh - ter, And greet your prom - ised king. Spread branch - es in his path - way And loud Ho - san - nas sing! He comes a - stride a don - key In

2. O Christ, though king they hailed you, They sent you out to die, For soon the songs of prais - es Were drowned by, "Cru - ci - fy!" They stripped a - way your gar - ments. They

3. But still you come a - mong us In cit - ies built with pride. You walk the streets of sor - row Where hate and greed di - vide. Re - deem us from our mad - ness, The

4. We shout a - gain, "Ho - san - na!" We hail you as our king! Christ, stir our wills to ac - tion To match the praise we sing. Send us where truth is threat - ened, Where

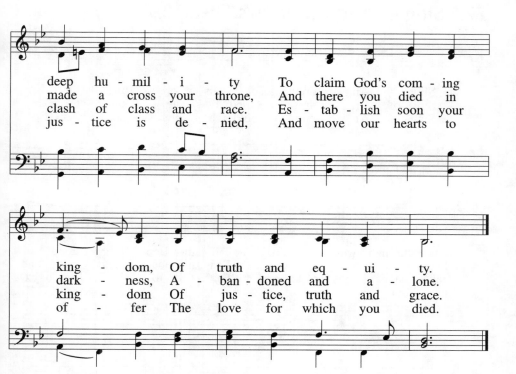

deep hu - mil - i - ty   To   claim God's com - ing
made   a   cross your throne,   And there you died   in
clash   of   class and   race.   Es - tab - lish soon your
jus - tice   is   de - nied,   And move   our hearts   to

king - dom,   Of   truth   and   eq - ui - ty.
dark - ness,   A - ban - doned   and   a - lone.
king - dom   Of   jus - tice,   truth   and   grace.
of - fer   The   love   for   which   you   died.

Text: Herman G. Stuempfle, b.1923, © 1997, GIA Publications, Inc.
Tune: ST. THEODULPH, 7 6 7 6 D; Melchior Teschner, 1584-1635

77 Sing of Andrew, John's Disciple

1. Sing of An - drew, John's dis - ci - ple, Led by
2. Sing of An - drew, called by Je - sus From the
3. Sing of An - drew, bold a - pos - tle, Sent to

faith through ways un - trod, Till the Bap - tist cried at
shores of Gal - i - lee, Leav - ing boats and nets and
make the gos - pel known, Faith - ful to his Lord's ex -

Jor - dan, "There be - hold the Lamb of God." Stirred by
kin - dred, Trust - ing in that "Fol - low me." When a
am - ple, Called to make a cross his own. So may

hear - ing this new teach - er, An - drew,
lad's small meal fed thou - sands, When in -
we who prize his mem - 'ry Hon - or

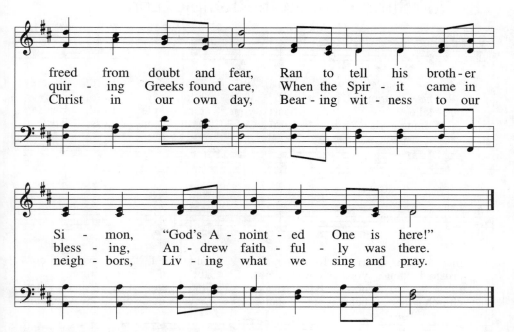

freed   from   doubt   and   fear,   Ran   to   tell   his   broth-er
quir - ing   Greeks found care,   When the   Spir - it   came in
Christ   in   our   own   day,   Bear - ing   wit - ness   to   our

Si - mon,   "God's A - noint - ed   One   is   here!"
bless - ing,   An - drew   faith - ful - ly   was   there.
neigh - bors,   Liv - ing   what   we   sing   and   pray.

Text: Carl P. Daw, Jr., b.1944, © 1987, Hope Publishing Co.
Tune: NETTLETON, 8 7 8 7 D; Wyeth's *Repository of Sacred Music, Pt. II,* 1813

78 You Strode Within the Temple, Lord

1. You strode with - in the Tem - ple, Lord, Where
2. The tem - ple of your bod - y, Lord, They
3. Make ev - 'ry heart your tem - ple, Lord, Each
4. Come, vis - it, Lord of right - eous - ness, The

mer - chants vied for gain And cried, "Your wares cor -
crushed when you were slain; But af - ter three days'
life a ho - ly place. For - give the sins that
church that bears your name. Drive out our fear and

rupt God's house, This place of prayer pro - fane!" With
sleep in death, God raised it up a - gain. And
flaw your plan, your pa - tient work de - face. In
un - be - lief, The pride that is our shame. Re -

cord - ed whip and fier - y wrath You
now you have a dwell - ing place On
love that does not shrink from truth These
new the life we share, O Christ, In

put God's foes to flight. They could not bear the
earth, in all its lands. Your peo - ple are your
tem - ples pu - ri - fy. And then in mer - cy,
love and prayer and praise. Then send us forth, our

search - ing beam Of your un - shield - ed light.
tem - ple, Lord, A house not made with hands.
Lord, re - main; Your Spir - it's gifts sup - ply.
strength re - stored, To serve you all our days.

Text: Herman G. Stuempfle, b.1923, © 2000, GIA Publications, Inc.
Tune: KINGSFOLD, CMD; English; harm. by Ralph Vaughan Williams, 1872-1958, © Oxford University Press, Inc.

79 God Our Author and Creator

1. God our Au - thor and Cre - a - tor, In whose life we find our own, Make our dai - ly wit - ness great - er, By our lives make your love known. Help us show how love em - brac - es Those whom

2. Like those first a - pos - tles, Sav - ior, Give us strength to love and serve: When our faint - ing spir - its wav - er, Fire our hearts and steel our nerve. Teach us wis - dom and com - pas - sion: Bid our

3. Keep us faith - ful, Ho - ly Spir - it, Help us bear the mes - sage true, That at last all lands may hear it: "God is love; Christ died for you." Join our lives in might - y cho - rus Till we

fear and greed down - trod: In all yearn - ing hearts and
rest - less thoughts be still; By your guid - ance help us
come from ev - 'ry place, With all those who went be -

fac - es Let us see a child of God.
fash - ion Lives con - formed un - to your will.
fore us, To the full - ness of God's grace.

Text: Carl P. Daw, Jr. b.1944, © 1987, Van Ness Press, Inc.
Tune: BEACH SPRING, 8 7 8 7D; attr. Benjamin Franklin White, 1844; harm. by Ronald A. Nelson, © 1978, *Lutheran Book of Worship*

80 God, Whose Purpose Is to Kindle

1. God,   whose pur - pose is   to   kin - dle:
2. God,   who   in   your   ho - ly   gos - pel
3. God,   who   still a   sword de - liv - ers

Now   ig - nite us   with your fire;
Wills   that   all   should tru - ly live,
Rath - er   than   a   plac - id peace,

While the   earth a - waits your burn - ing,
Make   us   sense our   share of   fail - ure,
With   your sharp - ened word dis - turb us,

With   your pas - sion us   in - spire.   O - ver - come our
Our   tran - quil - li - ty   for - give.   Teach us   cour - age
From   com - pla - cen - cy   re - lease!   Save us   now from

sin - ful calm-ness, Stir us with your sav - ing name;
as we strug-gle In all lib - er - at - ing strife;
sat - is - fac - tion, When we pri - vate - ly are free,

Bap - tize with your fier - y Spir - it,
Lift the small - ness of our vi - sion
Yet are un - dis - turbed in spir - it

Crown our lives with tongues of flame.
By your own a - bun - dant life.
By our neigh - bor's mis - er - y.

Text: David E. Trueblood, b.1900, © 1967, David Elton Trueblood
Tune: HOLY MANNA, 8 7 8 7 D; William Moore

81   As Servants Working an Estate

1. As ser - vants work - ing an es - tate Whose own - er is a - way, And whose re - turn they all a - wait Though no one knows the day, So none of us can name the hour, The
2. Our task is not to cal - cu - late What an - gels do not know, But faith - ful - ly to watch and wait And Christ's com - pas - sion show. So Not load - ing frag - ile hu - man schemes With
3. For Christ the Lord will sure - ly come, The king whom kings will fear, And with God's per - fect jus - tice plumb The jus - tice we do here, Re - veal - ing that the pres - ent age And
4. So guide, Lord Christ, our ev - 'ry choice That when our hearts shall hear Your step, your knock, your call - ing voice We will not hide in fear, But wel - come you from realms a - bove To

sea - son or the year When Christ with all of
hopes they can - not bear, We trust the prom - ise
ev - 'ry age that's past Are not the fin - al
your es - tate be - low, Where jus - tice, mer - cy,

heav - en's pow'r Will sud - den - ly ap - pear.
that re - deems The pres - ent from de - spair.
mor - al gauge That judg - es us at last.
peace and love A - bun - dant - ly will grow.

Text: Thomas H. Troeger, b.1945, © 1994, Oxford University Press, Inc.
Tune: KINGSFOLD, CMD; English; harm. by Ralph Vaughan Williams, 1872-1958, © Oxford University Press, Inc.

82 Word of God, When All Was Silent

1. Word of God, when all was si - lent,
2. Word made flesh, you came a - mong us
3. Word of Life, raised up in pow - er
4. Word of God, your call, un - si - lenced,
5. Praise the Word for life un - end - ing!

Source of all that was to be;
Shar - ing all our joy and pain,
From the tomb on Eas - ter morn,
Sounds through - out our pass - ing years,
Praise the Word for truth that heals!

With the Fa - ther and the Spir - it,
Help - ing, heal - ing, liv - ing, lov - ing,
Vic - tor o - ver death's do - min - ion,
Seek - ing, prob - ing, pen - e - trat - ing
Praise the Word that shines where dark - ness

One throughout e - ter - ni - ty:
Lamb of God, for sin - ners slain:
Bring - ing hope to souls for - lorn:
By its truth our doubts and fears:
God's un - dy - ing love con - ceals!

When you spoke the whole cre - a - tion
By your bod - y, bro - ken, bleed - ing,
Make our lives a new cre - a - tion
Speak to us un - til we hear you;
Praise the Word whose grace in - car - nate

Came to birth by your de - cree.
Make cre - a - tion whole a - gain.
By the Spir - it's gift re - born.
O - pen dulled and deaf - ened ears.
Still the heart of God re - veals!

Text: Herman G. Stuempfle, b.1923, © 2000, GIA Publications, Inc.
Tune: WESTMINSTER ABBEY, 8 7 8 7 8 7; adapt. from an anthem of Henry Purcell, 1659-1695

83 Not Alone, but Two by Two

1. Not a-lone, but two by two, Je - sus sent dis-
2. Have we still such dar - ing hearts? Can we claim their
3. Ho - ly Spir - it, breathe through us With your u - ni-

ci - ples out: Yoked to share their grow - ing faith,
faith and nerve? Do we tru - ly love the world
fy - ing might; Kin - dle cleans-ing, melt - ing flames

Spurred by cour-age, slowed by doubt. Tak - ing but a
Je - sus calls for us to serve? Can we plant a -
Till our frac-tured wills u - nite. Bind our hearts in

walk - ing stick, Mon - ey - less and san - dal - shod,
gain the seed Sown in mu - tual min - is - try,
mu - tual love, Par - a - dox that sets self free;

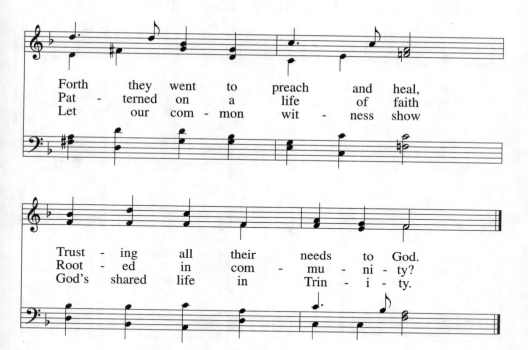

Forth they went to preach and heal,
Pat - terned on a life of faith
Let our com - mon wit - ness show

Trust - ing all their needs to God.
Root - ed in com - mu - ni - ty?
God's shared life in Trin - i - ty.

Text: Carl P. Daw, Jr., b.1944, © 1994, Hope Publishing Co.
Tune: ST. GEORGE'S WINDSOR, 7 7 7 7 D; George J. Elvey, 1816-1893

84   Rest, O Christ, from All Your Labor

1. Rest, O Christ, from all your la - bor;
2. Peace at last from all your an - guish,
3. Help us keep this sol - emn sab - bath
4. As, through part - ing Red Sea wa - ters,

Sleep with - in your bor - rowed tomb.
Wounds in hands and feet and side.
As we wait for Eas - ter dawn.
Is - rael marched to lib - er - ty,

Foes have cru - ci - fied and bound you
En - e - mies no long - er mock you,
Earth's dark night of sin is pass - ing;
So we pass through bap - tism's wa - ter,

Fast with - in death's nar - row room.
Scourged, a - ban - doned, cru - ci - fied.
Death's long reign will soon be gone.
Washed by grace, from sin set free.

1. Pi - late's guards stand watch - ing, wait - ing
2. Faith - ful wom - en gath - er spic - es,
3. Christ, in whom the new cre - a - tion
4. Je - sus, ris - en, liv - ing, reign - ing

1. Where they rolled the seal - ing stone.
2. Weep for you whom sin has slain.
3. Ris - es bright - er than the sun:
4. Now and through e - ter - ni - ty:

1. All un - seen an - oth - er watch - es:
2. Though they mourn, the God who guards you
3. May we, as we watch for morn - ing,
4. Grant that, through your life un - dy - ing,

1. God will not for - sake his own.
2. Will not let your death be vain.
3. Trust the vic - t'ry you have won.
4. We may live vic - tor - ious - ly.

Text: Herman G. Stuempfle, b.1923, © 1993, GIA Publications, Inc.
Tune: PLEADING SAVIOR, 8 7 8 7 D; Joshua Leavitt's *Christian Lyre*, 1830

85 We Come with Joy

1. We come with joy in Je - sus Christ, Who
2. A lit - tle bread is all we have, So
3. Like rip - ples in a pool, our gifts, How -

knows our hu - man need, Who, moved with pit - y
mea - ger our sup - ply— A lit - tle time, a
ev - er small they are, Will reach and heal a

for the world, Would ev - 'ry hun - ger feed,
lit - tle love Can hard - ly sat - is - fy.
need - y world, Will com - fort near and far.

Who blessed the fish and bar - ley loaves Till
But let us bring the best we have De -
For Christ will bless our bit of bread, The

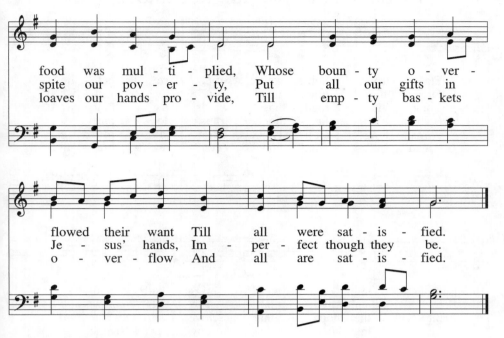

food   was   mul - ti - plied,   Whose   boun - ty   o - ver -
spite   our   pov - er - ty,   Put   all   our   gifts   in
loaves   our   hands   pro - vide,   Till   emp - ty   bas - kets

flowed   their   want   Till   all   were   sat - is - fied.
Je - sus'   hands,   Im - per - fect though they   be.
o - ver - flow   And   all   are   sat - is - fied.

Text: Delores Dufner, OSB, © 1994, GIA Publications, Inc.
Tune: FOREST GREEN, CMD; English; harm. by Ralph Vaughan Williams, 1872-1958, © Oxford University Press, Inc., alt.

86 Far From Home We Run Rebellious

1. Far from home we run, re - bel - lious,
2. Dreams that lured us on have van - ished;
3. Long the road that winds us home - ward,
4. Swift, a fa - ther runs to meet us,
5. Arms, long emp - ty, close a - round us,
6. Bread and wine for cel - e - bra - tion

Seek - ing cit - ies bright with dreams,
Free - dom's road has run its course.
Faint the hope that love still waits;
Bear - ing love that cov - ers shame.
Bind - ing hearts in warm em - brace.
On the ta - ble now are spread.

Cast - ing loose from love that claims us,
All that glit - tered now lies tar - nished,
Yet the feet that once were way - ward
Sin and guilt no more de - feat us;
Love we'd lost once more has found us,
Songs as - cend in jub - i - la - tion,

Crav - ing life that glit - ters, gleams.
Robbed of joy by guilt, re - morse.
Lead us toward fa - mil - iar gates.
Grace re - stores a home, a name.
Shines a - gain from face to face.
For we live who once were dead!

Text: Herman G. Stuempfle, b.1923, © 1993, GIA Publications, Inc.
Tune: GOTT WILL'S MACHEN, 8 7 8 7; Johann Ludwig Steiner, 1723

Christ Has Promised to Be Present   87

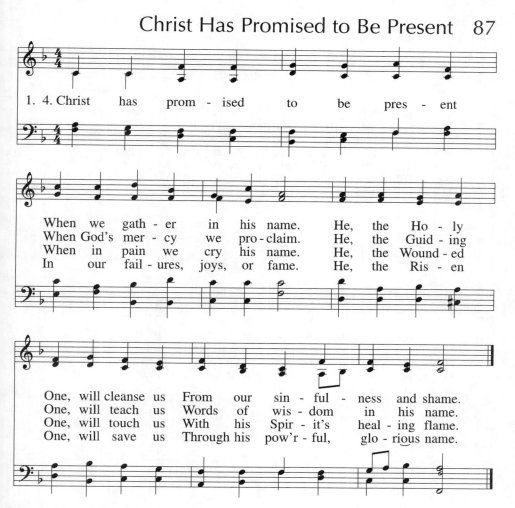

1. 4. Christ has prom - ised to be pres - ent

When we gath - er in his name. He, the Ho - ly
When God's mer - cy we pro - claim. He, the Guid - ing
When in pain we cry his name. He, the Wound - ed
In our fail - ures, joys, or fame. He, the Ris - en

One, will cleanse us From our sin - ful - ness and shame.
One, will teach us Words of wis - dom in his name.
One, will touch us With his Spir - it's heal - ing flame.
One, will save us Through his pow'r - ful, glo - rious name.

Text: Rae E. Whitney, © 1994, Selah Publishing Co., Inc.
Tune: STUTTGART, 8 7 8 7; *Psalmodia Sacra*, 1715; adapt. and harm. by William Henry Havergal, 1793-1870, alt.

88 Welcome, All You Noble Saints

1. Wel-come, all you no-ble saints of old, As
2. El-ders, mar-tyrs, all are fall-ing down;
3. Beg-gars, lame, and har-lots al-so here; Re -
4. Who is this who spreads the vic-t'ry feast?
5. Here he gives him-self to us as bread:
6. Wor-ship in the pres-ence of the Lord. With
7. When at last this earth shall pass a-way. When

now be-fore your ver-y eyes un-fold. The
Proph-ets, pa-tri-archs are gath-'ring 'round. What
pen-tant pub-li-cans are draw-ing near;
Who is this who makes our war-ring cease?
Here, as wine, we drink the blood he shed.
joy-ful songs and hearts in one ac-cord. And
Je-sus and his bride are one to stay. The

won-ders all so long a-go fore-told: The
an-gels long to see now we have found.
Way-ward sons come home with-out a fear.
Je-sus, ris-en Sav-ior, Prince of Peace. In
Born to die, we eat and live in-stead!
let our host at ta-ble be a-dored.
feast of love is just be-gun that day.

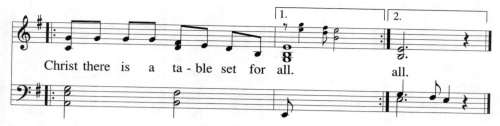

Christ there is a ta-ble set for all. all.

Text: Robert J. Stamps
Tune: CENEDIUS, Irregular; Robert J. Stamps
© 1972, Dawn Treader Music

Waken, O Sleeper 89

1. Wak - en O sleep - er, wake and rise, Sal -
2. Let us pre - pare to face the day Of
3. Watch then and pray, we can - not know The
4. Then shall the na - tions gath - er round To

va - tion's day is near, And let the dawn of
judge - ment and of grace, To live as peo - ple
mo - ment or the hour, When Christ, un - her - ald -
learn his ways of peace, When spears to prun - ing -

light and truth Dis - pel the night of fear.
of the light, And per - fect truth em - brace.
ed, will come With life - re - new - ing pow'r.
hooks are turned, And all our con - flicts cease.

Text: Michael Forster, © 1993, Kevin Mayhew, Ltd
Tune: ST. FLAVIAN, CM; John's *Day Psalter*, 1562; harm. based on the original faux-bourdon setting.

90 Good News

Verses

Capo 5: (Am) Dm   (G) C   (C) F

1. When Je - sus worked here on earth he
2. The eld - ers of the syn - a - gogue were
3. The way he lived was proof of it: he
4. So pass it on to - day, good friend: the

(Dm) Gm   (C) F   (G) C   (Am) Dm   (G) C

preached in his home - town, I - sa - iah's hopes
shocked by Mar - y's son, that he was des -
qui - et - ed our strife. The cross it - self he
mes - sage is the same. De - liv - 'rance Christ a -

(C) F   (Dm) Gm   (F) B♭   (C) F

now ful - filled, those claims of great re - nown.
tined to be the Christ for ev - 'ry - one.
would not flee e'en though it cost his life.
lone can give, for this to earth he came.

Refrain (C) F   (Dm) Gm   (C) F

To bring good news to the need - y, to make the blind to

(Dm) Gm   (Am) Dm   (G) C   (C) F

see, the bro - ken hearts healed a - gain, to

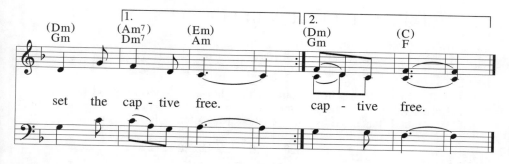

set the cap - tive free.   cap - tive free.

Text: Howard S. Olson
Tune: Almaz Belihu; Yemissrach Dimts Literature Program, Ethiopia
© 1993, Howard S. Olson

What Shall We Say God's Realm Is Like   91

1. What shall we say God's realm is like, What
2. God's realm is like a mus - tard seed, The
3. God's king - dom, like a mus - tard plant, For

par - a - ble can tell, E - ter - nal truth, in
small - est seed of all. Yet, when it's plant - ed
shel - t'ring peace is made. It's wel - c'ming branch - es

sim - ple words, And il - lus - trate it well?
in the earth, It grows up, full and tall.
spread for all To rest with - in its shade.

Text: John A. Dalles, © 2000, GIA Publications, Inc.
Tune: LAND OF REST, CM; American; harm. by Annabel M. Buchanan, 1888-1983, © 1938, J. Fisher and Bro.

92 Tell It! Tell It Out with Gladness

1. Tell it! Tell it out with glad-ness— God's good news to
2. Lord, we thank thee for the treas-ure Hid with-in the
3. "Go and teach," thus spoke the Mas-ter, Ris - en vic - tor

ev - 'ry land, Sin for-giv-en, lives trans-fig-ured,
sa - cred page. We would be thy faith-ful her-alds
from the grave. Still he gives this great com-mis-sion

All in God's great lov - ing plan. In the Book is
To our deep-ly trou-bled age; We would pub-lish
To his faith-ful ones, and brave. Go and tell the

found the wit-ness To his might-y acts of yore:
thy sal-va-tion, Ev - er on thy side to stand,
gos-pel sto-ry Of what all through Christ can be.

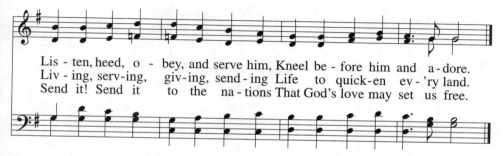

Lis - ten, heed, o - bey, and serve him, Kneel be - fore him and a - dore.
Liv - ing, serv-ing, giv-ing, send - ing Life to quick-en ev - 'ry land.
Send it! Send it to the na - tions That God's love may set us free.

Text: Georgia Harkness, 1891-1974, © 1966, The Hymn Society. Administered by Hope Publishing Co.
Tune: HYMN TO JOY, 8 7 8 7 D; arr. from Ludwig van Beethoven, 1770-1827, by Edward Hodges, 1796-1867.

We Sing Your Praise, O Christ   93

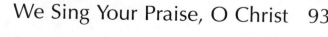

1. We sing your praise, O Christ, With
2. When eyes are fixed a - bove Where
3. We fall up - on our knees And
4. Let praise we of - fer you Be

hearts ex - alt - ed high. For - give us when we
you in glo - ry reign, Lord, low - er them to
fold our hands in prayer. Lord, o - pen them that
ech - oed in our deeds. Let love of you be

fail to hear Our neigh-bor's an - guished cry.
earth a - gain To see a world in pain.
grace re - ceived Be grace we glad - ly share.
man - i - fest In serv - ing oth - er's needs.

Text: Herman G. Stuempfle, b.1923, © 1997, GIA Publications, Inc.
Tune: FESTAL SONG, SM; William H. Walter

94 O Christ, Unsheathe Your Sword

1. O Christ, un - sheathe your sword; Strike e - vil at its root. Let pride and greed no long - er yield Op - pres - sion's bit - ter fruit.

2. O Prince of Peace, con - tend For truth that sets us free. Do bat - tle on be - half of all En - slaved by tyr - an - ny.

3. You hurled the spear of love A - gainst in - iq - ui - ty; And yet, when sol - diers rained their blows, You bore them pa - tient - ly.

4. Lord, arm your church with truth; E - quip us with your grace. Then send us forth by your com - mand To heal our wound - ed race.

5. Nor let our cour - age fail Where jus - tice is de - nied, And give us strength to bear the cross Where life is cru - ci - fied.

Text: Herman G. Stuempfle, b.1923, © 1997, GIA Publications, Inc.
Tune: FESTAL SONG, SM; William H. Walter

1. O day of God, draw nigh In beau - ty and in pow'r, Come with thy time - less judg-ment now To match our pres - ent hour.

2. Bring to our trou - bled minds, Un - cer - tain and a - fraid, The qui - et of a stead-fast faith, Calm of a call o - beyed.

3. Bring jus - tice to our land, That all may dwell se - cure, And fine - ly build for days to come Foun - da - tions that en - dure.

4. Bring to our world of strife Thy sov - 'reign word of peace, That war may haunt the earth no more And des - o - la - tion cease.

5. O day of God, draw nigh As at cre - a - tion's birth, Let there be light a - gain, and set Thy judg-ments in the earth.

Text: Robert Belgarnie Young Scott, b.1899
Tune: SOUTHWELL, SM; Damon's *Psalmes*, 1579

96   The Reign of God

1. The reign of God, like farm-er's field, Bears weeds a - long with wheat; The good and bad are in - ter - twined Till har - vest is com - plete.

2. Like mus - tard tree, the reign of God From ti - ny seed will spread, Till birds of ev - 'ry feath - er come To nest, and there be fed.

3. Though hid - den now, the reign of God May, yet un - no - ticed, grow; From deep with - in it ris - es up, Like yeast in swell - ing dough.

4. The reign of God is come in Christ; The reign of God is near. A - blaze a - mong us, kind - ling hearts, The reign of God is here!

Text: Delores Dufner, OSB, © 1995, Sisters of St. Benedict
Tune: MCKEE, CM; African American; adapt. by Harry T. Burleigh, 1866-1949

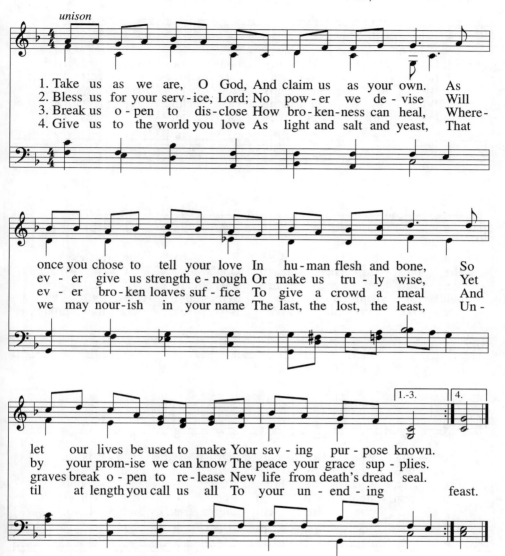

1. Take us as we are, O God, And claim us as your own. As once you chose to tell your love In hu-man flesh and bone, So let our lives be used to make Your sav-ing pur-pose known.

2. Bless us for your serv-ice, Lord; No pow-er we de-vise Will ev-er give us strength e-nough Or make us tru-ly wise, Yet by your prom-ise we can know The peace your grace sup-plies.

3. Break us o-pen to dis-close How bro-ken-ness can heal, Where-ev-er bro-ken loaves suf-fice To give a crowd a meal And graves break o-pen to re-lease New life from death's dread seal.

4. Give us to the world you love As light and salt and yeast, That we may nour-ish in your name The last, the lost, the least, Un-til at length you call us all To your un-end-ing feast.

Text: Carl P. Daw, Jr., b.1944, © 1995, Hope Publishing Co.
Tune: ENDLESS FEAST, 7 6 8 6 8 6; Alfred V. Fedak, © 1995, Selah Publishing Co.

98 Our Savior's Infant Cries Were Heard

1. Our sav - ior's in - fant cries were heard And
2. In Jo - seph's arms, at Mar - y's breast, While
3. By trust - ing Christ to hu - man care God
4. Who - ev - er calms a child by night Or
5. For Christ who was a ref - u - gee From

met by hu - man love Be - fore he preached one
Her - od's vio - lence spread, God's love by hu - man
blessed for - ev - er - more The care of chil - dren
guides a youth by day Serves him whose birth by
Her - od and his sword Is seek - ing now through

sav - ing word Or prayed to God a - bove.
love was blessed, Pro - tect - ed, nur - tured, fed.
ev - 'ry - where—The bruised, the lost, the poor.
lan - tern light Was on a bed of hay.
us to be Our chil - dren's friend and Lord.

Text: Thomas H. Troeger, b.1945, © 1994, Oxford University Press, Inc.
Tune: WINCHESTER OLD, CM; Thomas Est; harm. from *Hymns Ancient and Modern*, 1922

1. Let kings and proph-ets yield their name To Je - sus, true A -
2. But God re - veals to search - ing faith The truths that pi - ous
3. Give us, O God, the grace to know The lim - its of our

noint - ed One, For whom a na - tion looked in hope Yet
dog - mas hide: When Je - sus asked the twelve his name, Blunt
cer - tain - ty: Help us, like Pe - ter, to de - clare The

failed to see that God had done A strange and un - ex -
Pe - ter stepped forth and re - plied In words that seemed both
still - un - fold - ing mys - ter - y Of One who reigns though

pect - ed thing: God sent a ser - vant, not a king.
right and odd: "You are Mes - si - ah, Son of God."
sac - ri - ficed, Our Lamb and Shep - herd, Je - sus Christ.

Text: Carl P. Daw, Jr., b.1944, © 1990, Hope Publishing Co.
Tune: MELITA, 8 8 8 8 8 88; John Bacchus Dykes, 1861

100 When the Lord in Glory Comes

1. When the Lord in glo - ry comes not the
   shout the heav - ens raise, not the
(2.) Lord is seen a - gain not the
   pomp and pow'r a - lone, not the
(3.) Lord to hu - man eyes shall be -
   man by all de - nied, not the

trum - pets, not the drums, not the an - them, not the
cho - rus, not the praise, not the si - lenc - es sub -
glo - ries of his reign, not the light - nings through the
splen-dours of his throne, not his robe and di - a -
stride our nar - row skies, not the child of hum - ble
vic - tim cru - ci - fied, but the God who died to

psalm, not the thun - der, not the calm, not the
lime, not the sounds of space and
storm, not the ra - diance of his form, not his
dems, not the gold and not the
birth, not the car - pen - ter of earth, not the
save, but the vic - tor of the

Text: Timothy Dudley-Smith, b.1926, © 1967, Hope Publishing Co.
Tune: ST. JOHN'S, 77 77 77 D; Bob Morre, b.1962, © 1993, GIA Publications, Inc.

This hymn may be sung by choir or cantor, with the congregation entering each stanza at the asterisk (*).

101   In a Lowly Manger Born

1. In a low - ly man - ger born, Hum - ble life be -
2. Vis - it - ing the lone and lost, Stead - y - ing the
3. Then, to res - cue you and me, Je - sus died up -

gun in scorn; Un - der Jo - seph's watch - ful eye,
tem - pest-tossed, Giv - ing of him - self in love,
on the tree. See in him God's love re - vealed;

Je - sus grew as you and I; Knew the suf - f'rings
Call - ing minds to things a - bove. Sin - ners glad - ly
By his Pas - sion we are healed. Now he lives in

of the weak, Knew the pa - tience of the meek,
hear his call; Pub - li - cans be - fore him fall,
glo - ry bright, Lives a - gain in pow'r and might;

Hun - gered as but poor folk can;
For in him new life be - gan;
Come and take the path he trod,

This is he. Be - hold the man!
This is he. Be - hold the man!
Son of Mar - y, Son of God.

Text: Koh Yuki; tr. hymnal version, © 1978, *Lutheran Book of Worship*
Tune: ABERYSTWYTH, 77 77 D; Joseph Parry, 1841-1903

102 Martha, Mary, Waiting, Weeping

1. Mar-tha, Mar - y, wait-ing, weep - ing, Bowed be-
2. Je - sus spoke to Mar-tha's griev - ing, "Res - ur-
3. Je - sus, res - ur - rect-ed, giv - ing Life to

neath the weight of gloom, Kept their watch where Laz-'rus,
rec - tion, Life, am I! All who hear my Word, be-
all you name your own: Help us know in hours of

sleep - ing, Lay with - in a rock sealed tomb. Je - sus,
liev - ing, Live with me, al - though they die." Then to
griev - ing We have not been left a - lone. Come, when

late in com-ing, met them, Shed with them com -
Laz - 'rus' tomb he led them, Called their broth - er
doubt and fear as - sail us; Join our jour - ney

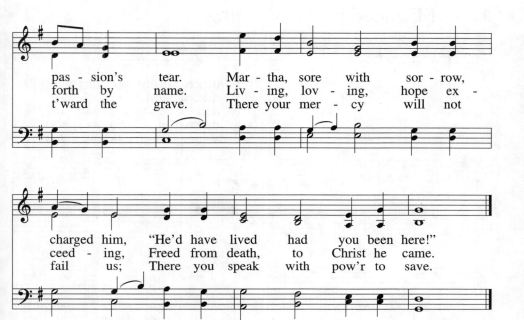

pas - sion's   tear.   Mar - tha, sore   with   sor - row,
forth   by   name.   Liv - ing, lov - ing,   hope ex -
t'ward   the   grave.   There your mer - cy   will not

charged him,   "He'd have lived   had   you been here!"
ceed - ing,   Freed from death,   to   Christ he came.
fail   us;   There you speak   with   pow'r to save.

Text: Herman G. Stuempfle, b.1923, © 1997, GIA Publications, Inc.
Tune: BEACH SPRING, 8 7 8 7 D; *The Sacred Harp,* 1844; harm. by Ronald A. Nelson, © 1978, *Lutheran Book of Worship*

103 I Danced in the Morning

1. I danced in the morn-ing when the
2. I danced for the scribe and the
3. I danced on the Sab-bath and I
4. I danced on a Fri-day when the
5. They cut me down and I

world was be-gun, And I danced in the moon and the
phar - i - see, But they would not dance, and they
cured the lame: The ho - ly peo - ple said it
sky turned black; It's hard to dance with the
leapt up high; I am the life that - 'll

stars and the sun, And I came down from heav - en and I
would-n't fol - low me; I danced for the fish - er - men, for
was a shame. They whipped and they stripped and they
dev - il on your back. They bur - ied my bod - y and they
nev - er, nev - er die; I'll live in you if you'll

danced on the earth; At Beth - le - hem I had my birth.
James and John; They came with me and the dance went on.
hung me high, And left me there on a Cross to die.
thought I'd gone; But I am the dance and I still go on.
live in me: I am the Lord of the Dance, said he.

Dance then wher - ev - er you may be; I am the Lord of the

Dance, said he, And I'll lead you all, wher - ev - er you may be, And I'll

1.- 4.

5.

lead you all in the Dance, said he. Dance, said he.

Text: Sydney Carter, b.1915, © 1963, Stainer & Bell Ltd., London, England. Administered by Hope Publishing Co.
Tune: LORD OF THE DANCE, Irregular; adapt. from a traditional Shaker melody; harm. by Sydney Carter, b.1915, © 1963, Stainer & Bell Ltd., London, England. Administered by Hope Publishing Co.

104 Eternal Christ, Who, Kneeling

1. E - ter - nal Christ, who, kneel - ing When
2. But we have of - ten slight - ed The
3. Ac - cept our deep con - tri - tion For
4. In this our gen - er - a - tion Make

earth - ly tasks were done, Turned un - to God ap -
ties de - signed to hold Your fol - low - ers u -
all our sun - d'ring ways Which still dis - rupt your
fruit - ful, Lord, our search For rec - on - cil - i -

peal - ing, "That they may all be one,"
nit - ed With - in one com - mon fold.
mis - sion, Which mock our words of praise.
a - tion Of all with - in your church.

We thank you for your vi - sion Of
Writ dark on his - t'ry's pag - es We
Lord, may your Spir - it guide us That
Re - deemed from her un - fit - ness, Lord,

u - ni - ty un - torn, Of faith with - out di -
see, O Lord, with shame, The strife which through the
we may find, be - yond The things which still di -
may the church, your bridge, As one pro - claim her

vi - sion With which your church was born.
a - ges Has marred your chur - ch's name.
vide us, Love's all - em - brac - ing bond.
wit - ness, As one with you a - bide.

Text: William W. Reid, Jr., b.1923, © 1976, The Hymn Society. Administered by Hope Publishing Co.
Tune: NYLAND, 7 6 7 6 D; Finnish Melody; adapt. and harm. by David Evans, 1874-1948, © Oxford University Press, Inc.

105   If Christ Is Charged with Madness

1. If   Christ is charged with mad - ness, It's   mad - ness that's di -
2. Thus when Christ seized and plun - dered The   de - mons' dark do -
3. Christ spoke to   all   this   rant - ing, A   viv - id,   lu - cid
4. De - spite his deft ex - plain - ing, Christ still ap - peared dis -
5. Yet   earth needs heav - en's mad - ness To   seize with grace and

vine,   A   vi - sion - ar - y   glad - ness This
main,   His friends and foes both won - dered If
word   A   par - a - ble sup - plant - ing The
traught To   guard - i - ans main - tain - ing Ac -
bind   The guilt, the hurt, the sad - ness, The

world can - not con - fine,   The   mad - ness of con -
he   were not in - sane.   They charged his soul was
char - ges he had heard.   "A   house that is di -
cept - ed bounds of thought.   The   force of faith in
fear and hate that blind.   In - trude, O Christ, im -

ceiv - ing What no one else can see, Then
riv - en, His heart and mind pos - sessed By
vid - ed, A king - dom, soul or land With
ac - tion Seems mad - ness to each age And
pas - sioned With mad - ness that's di - vine Up -

act - ing and be - liev - ing So it will come to be.
forc - es he had driv - en From those who were dis - tressed.
rag - ing wars in - side it Can - not sur - vive and stand."
of - ten the re - ac - tion Is fear dis - guised as rage.
on the world we've fash - ioned And give it your de - sign.

Text: Thomas H. Troeger, b.1945, © 1994, Oxford University Press, Inc.
Tune: AURELIA, 7 6 7 6 D; Samuel Sebastian Wesley, 1810-1876

106　At Evening When the Sun Was Set

1. At eve - ning when the sun was set The
2. Then lat - er in the midst of night He
3. But when they saw him walk - ing by, Their
4. For they were sore - ly trou - bled then, To
5. He climbed in - to the boat with them And

ship was out to sea, And Je - sus saw them
walked up - on the sea, Be - side the boat, the
Lord up - on the sea, They feared that they had
see their Lord pass by Though Je - sus quick - ly
then the winds did cease, But they were sore a -

from the land Out in the winds and sea.
Sav - ior walked Up - on the storm - y sea.
seen a ghost, They cried out fear - ful - ly.
spoke to them, "O fear not, it is I!"
mazed at him Whose pres - ence stilled the sea.

Text: Gracia Grindal, © 1993, Selah Publishing Co., Inc.
Tune: LAND OF REST, CM; American; harm. by Annabel M. Buchanan, 1888-1983, © 1938, J. Fisher and Bro.

unison

1. Still as dew falls on the mead - ow,
2. Gen - tle as a spring - time show - er,
3. Qui - et lies the moon - lit pas - ture,
4. Stand with Jo - seph, ev - er faith - ful,
5. Songs of an - gels stream through star - light,
6. Kneel with shep - herds by the man - ger

Soft - ly as the seed in sod, Si - lent as a
Giv - ing as the fruit - ful earth, Grace - ful as a
Calm the watch - ing stars a - bove. God draws near in
While his qui - et watch he keeps. Pon - der, as you
Spill up - on the si - lent earth. Star - tled shep - herds
Near the sleep - ing child so poor. Know that none can

pass - ing shad - ow, Comes the mys - ter - y of God.
sum - mer flow - er, Mar - y waits the ho - ly birth.
hu - man ves - ture, Touch - es earth with heav - en's love.
keep your vig - il: God in flesh a - mong us sleeps!
bathed in fire - light Hear ce - les - tial sounds of mirth.
be a stran - ger Where such love un - bars the door.

Text: Herman G. Stuempfle, b.1923
Tune: PEACEFUL COMING, 8 7 8 7; Perry Nelson
© 1997, World Library Publications

108 From the Father's Throne on High

1. From the Fa-ther's throne on high
2. Dark-ened be the day at noon
3. An-cient pow'rs of sin and death
4. So be-hold the prom-ised sign,
5. Come then, Lord, in light and pow'r,

Christ re-turns to
When the stars of
Shake to hear the
Sky and sea by
At whose word the

rule and reign.
heav-en fall:
trum-pet blown;
tu-mult riv'n,
worlds be-gan;

Child of earth, he came to die;
Earth and sky and sun and moon—
From the winds' re-mot-est breath
And the King of kings di-vine
In the un-ex-pect-ed hour

Judge of all he comes a-gain.
Cloud-y dark-ness cov-ers all.
God will gath-er in his own.
Com-ing in the clouds of heav'n.
Come in glo-ry, Son of man!

Text: Timothy Dudley-Smith, b.1926, © 1987, Hope Publishing Co.
Tune: HEINLEIN, 7 7 7 7; attr. to Martin Herbst, 1654-1681

Show Me Your Hands, Your Feet, Your Side   109

1. Show me your hands, your feet, your side; I will not be de-ceived. Un-less I see, how can I trust The news that I've re-ceived?

2. Fear not! Let peace be in your soul. Reach out and touch and know I died and yet I am a-live With wounds that ev-er show.

3. Not e-ven Eas-ter takes a-way The marks that Je-sus bears. The Ris-en Christ still wears the wounds Of scourge and nail and spear.

4. So blessed are those who have not seen Yet cry, "My Lord and God!" Who touch earth's pain in Je-sus' name And tell good news a-broad.

Text: Sylvia Dunstan, 1955-1993, © 1991, GIA Publications, Inc.
Tune: DETROIT, CM; Supplement to *Kentucky Harmony*, 1820; harm. by Gerald H. Knight, 1908-1979, © The Royal School of Church Music

110   Lord of Lords, Adored by Angels

1. Lord of lords, a - dored by an - gels, Is that you with
2. As you shed your earth - ly gar - ments, So you laid a -
3. Moved by your de - vo - tion t'ward us, Hon - ored to be
4. Serv - ing Sav - ior, Mod - el Ser - vant, For the joy you

towel and ba - sin Wash - ing your dis - ci - ples' feet!?
side your glo - ry, So you shed your life as well.
called your ser - vants, We have joined you in your Way.
set be - fore us, Make your Way our his - to - ry,

Like the Twelve, we stare in won - der, Je - sus, Word of
Let the tow - el and the ba - sin Be the sym - bols
Hes - i - tant, we gird the tow - el, Fill the bowl with
Till we hear your com - men - da - tion: "Well done, good and

God e - ter - nal, Do you stoop to wash ours too!?
of our serv - ice; Let your mind be in us all.
cleans-ing Wa - ter, And be - gin to know your joy.
faith - ful ser - vant, Come and share my joy with me!"

Text: Jaroslav J. Vajda, b.1919, © 1988, Concordia Publishing House
Tune: STABAT MATER, 88 7; *Mainz Gesangbuch*, 1661; harm. by Richard Proulx, b.1937, © 1986, GIA Publications, Inc.

1. God is u-nique and one: Mak - er, sus-tain - er, Lord!
2. Love came to earth in Christ, Our com-mon life to share,
3. The Ho - ly Spir - it moves Peo - ple to trace God's plan,
4. He shall for ev - er reign, Rul - er of time and space,

Pat - terns of life were spun By God's cre - a - tive
Choos - ing to be the least, Will - ing a cross to
This in - spi - ra - tion proves More than the mind can
God in the midst of life, Seen in the hu - man

word. Of God's in - ten - tion, love and care We
bear. He died, he rose, that we might live And
span. Each lis - t'ning heart is led to find The
face. We give ex - pres - sion to our creed By

are with grow - ing trust a - ware.
all our love, re - spond - ing, give.
will of God for hu - man - kind.
love in thought, in word and deed.

Text: Fred Kaan, b.1929, alt., © 1968, Hope Publishing Co.
Tune: LITTLE CORNARD, 6 6 6 6 88; Martin Shaw, 1875-1958, © 1915, J. Curwen and Sons Ltd.

112 God in His Wisdom, for Our Learning

1. God in his wis - dom, for our learn - ing,
2. Sym - bol and sto - ry, song and say - ing,
3. Come then with prayer and con - tem - pla - tion,

Gave his in - spired and ho - ly word:
Life - bear - ing truths for heart and mind,
See how in Scrip - ture Christ is known;

Prom - ise of Christ, for our dis - cern - ing,
God in his sov - 'reign grace dis - play - ing
Won - der a - new at such sal - va - tion

By which our souls are moved and stirred,
Ten - der - est care for hu - man - kind,
Here in these sa - cred pag - es shown;

Find - ing our hearts with - in us burn - ing
Je - sus our Lord this love por - tray - ing,
Lift ev - 'ry heart in ad - o - ra - tion,

When, as of old, his voice is heard.
O - pen our eyes to seek and find.
Chil - dren of God by grace a - lone!

Text: Timothy Dudley-Smith, b.1926, © 1997, Hope Publishing Co.
Tune: FRAGRANCE, 9 8 9 8 9 8; French Traditional Carol, arr. Martin Fallas Shaw, 1875, 1958, © Oxford University Press, Inc.

113   Baited, the Question Rose

1. Bait - ed,   the   ques - tion   rose
2. "Whose im - age   does   it   bear,
3. May   we   dis - cern,   O   God,

From   some - where   in   the   crowd:
Whose   name   and   ti - tles   tell?"
Your   dai - ly   gifts   of   grace;

"Teach - er,   you   tru - ly   know   God's way;   Is
"Cae - sar's,   of course,"   they   smug - ly   said   And
Show   us   your   im - age   fresh - ly   coined   In

pay - ing   tax   al - lowed?"
thought   they   an - swered   well.
ev - 'ry   heart   and   face.

Je - sus per - ceived their trap:
"Give Cae - sar what is his;
Help us fit trib - ute yield

"Why do you test me so?" Bring
God, what is God's a - lone." Strong
Through prayers and hymns we raise, But

here the coin the tax re - quires, And
words, con - vinc - ing and pro - found, Like
most of all by deeds of love To

see what it will show."
truth al - read - y known.
give you thanks and praise.

Text: Carl P. Daw, Jr., b.1944, © 1996, Hope Publishing Co.
Tune: MERCER STREET, SMD; Malcolm Williamson, © 1975

114 Chosen and Sent by the Father

1. Cho - sen and sent by the Fa - ther be -
2. He con - quered death and the grave, and our
3. He will be in you, be - fore and be -
4. When you have worked till life's end and his
5. Sav - ior and Lord of our lives, for your

fore earth's cre - a - tion, Christ came from
foe is de - feat - ed; Now to earth's
hind and be - side you; All that you
man - date com - plet - ed, Then at his
call we a - dore you; All that we

heav - en in mer - cy to bring us sal - va -
end must the sto - ry of hope be re - peat -
need he has pledged by his blood to pro - vide
side by the throne of his glo - ry be seat -
are we would of - fer in wor - ship be - fore

tion; Now he sends you God's might - y plan to pur -
ed; So he sends you— Dai - ly his con - quest re -
you; Thus he sends you— Prove that his prom - ise is
ed; But till that day His last com - mand-ment o -
you; Read - y to go, Read - y your full - ness to

sue: Go in the strength of his Spir - it!
new: Live in the strength of his Spir - it!
true: Strong in the strength of his Spir - it!
bey, Strength-ened in might by his Spir - it!
know, Read - y to serve by your Spir - it!

Text: Margaret Clarkson, © 1974, Singspiration Music/ASCAP.
Tune: LOBE DEN HERREN, 14 14 47 8; *Stralsund Gesangbuch*, 1665

The Empty-Handed Fishermen 115

1. The emp - ty - hand - ed fish - er - men, The net that
2. There's break - fast wait - ing on the shore, With bread and
3. Now as we gath - er in this place, Our emp - ti -

fills when cast a - gain: Who shows a - bun - dance
fish up - on a fire. Who stands and wel - comes
ness is touched by grace. Who coun - sels, wel - comes,

with a word? None dare to ask; it is the Lord.
with a word? None dare to ask; it is the Lord.
feeds, and more? Who dares to ask? It is the Lord!

Text: Richard Leach, © 1994, Selah Publishing Co., Inc.
Tune: PUER NOBIS, LM; adapt. by Michael Praetorius, 1571-1621

116 Return, Redeemer God

1. Re - turn, Re - deem - er God, With judge-ment and with heal - ing: Our way - ward hearts re - store, Your light and truth re - veal - ing. O leave us not a - lone, Nor let us go a - stray, But

2. Here let us wait and pray To greet the Lord re - turn - ing, As watch - ers in the night With bea - cons ev - er burn - ing: For none can know the hour, His peo - ple long to see, When

3. May grace and peace be ours, From God the Fa - ther flow - ing, Through Je - sus Christ, our Lord, His per - fect truth be - stow - ing. This Fel - low - ship we share, The Fa - ther and the Son, Who

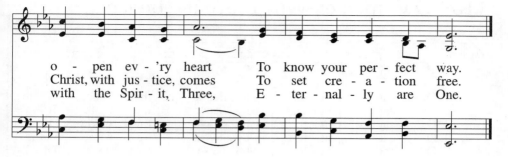

o - pen ev - 'ry heart   To know your per - fect   way.
Christ, with jus - tice, comes   To set cre - a - tion free.
with   the Spir - it, Three,   E - ter - nal - ly   are   One.

Text: Michael Forster, © 1993, Kevin Mayhew, Ltd.
Tune: NUN DANKET, 6 7 6 7 6 6 6 6; Johann Crüger, 1598-1662; harm. by A. Gregory Murray, OSB, 1905-1992

Let Justice Flow like Streams 117

1. Let   jus - tice   flow   like streams   Of
2. Let   right - eous - ness   roll   on   As
3. So   may   God's plumb line, straight,   De -

spar - kling wa - ter,   pure,   En - a - bling growth, re -
oth - ers' cares we   heed,   An ev - er - flow - ing
fine   our meas - ure   true,   And jus - tice, right, and

fresh - ing life, A - bun - dant, cleans - ing, sure.
stream of faith Trans - lat - ed in - to   deed.
peace per - vade This world our whole life through.

Text: Jane Parker Huber, b.1926, © 1984; admin. by Westminster John Knox Press
Tune: ST. THOMAS, SM; Aaron Williams; harm. by Lowell Mason, 1792-1872

118 O Carpenter, Why Leave the Bench

1. O car - pen - ter, why leave the bench Where
2. O car - pen - ter, why leave the tools To
3. O car - pen - ter, why leave the world Of
4. O car - pen - ter, why leave re - pairs With
5. O car - pen - ter, who else could do The

wood yields to your art, And take in - stead, to
car - ry out your plans, And go in - stead to
ta - ble, bed, and house, To face the em - pire's
wood and clamp and glue, To rise from death and
work that you have done? What can we do but

try your skill, The ston - y hu - man heart?
do God's work With emp - ty, o - pen hands?
car - pen - try, To lift a Ro - man cross?
seek in - stead To make the whole world new?
sing your praise, O Sav - ior, Mar - y's son!

Text: Richard Leach, © 1996, Selah Publishing Co., Inc.
Tune: LAND OF REST, CM; American; harm. by Annabel M. Buchanan, 1888-1983, © 1938, J. Fisher and Bro.

1. Famed though the world's great cit - ies be, Yet none can
2. More daz - zling than the dawn - ing sun, This star that
3. They who have lis - tened to earth's ways, Who long have
4. Pros - trate be - fore the throne of grace, They of - fer
5. Earth's sa - cred gifts speak mys - ter - ies: In - cense God's
6. The ma - gi, find - ing all they sought, Then trav - eled

Beth - le - hem ex - cel, For now there dawns God's
blaz - es at Christ's birth Pro - claims to all the
stud - ied heav - en's stars, Come seek - ing Wis - dom's
gifts both choice and rare: Gifts God first gave our
ho - li - ness ex - tolled, God's sov - 'reign realm the
home a dif - f'rent way; For noth - ing now re -

death - less day On Gen - tiles as on Is - ra - el.
wait - ing world: Our God en - fleshed up - on this earth.
ho - ly source—Their route a dif - f'rent one from ours.
moth - er earth, Her gold, her frank - in - cense and myrrh.
gold pro-claimed, But myrrh the cross and death fore - told.
mained the same In light of what they found this day.

Text: Aelred-Seton Shanley, © 1999
Tune: PUER NOBIS, LM; adapt. by Michael Praetorius, 1571-1621

120 As He Gathered at His Table

1. As he gath-ered at his ta-ble
2. As he took the tow'l and ba-sin,
3. As he blessed the bread and broke it,
4. As he took the cup and shared it,
5. As they sang a hymn to-geth-er,
6. As he went in-to the gar-den
7. Though this feast be one of sym-bols,

Those who
Not as
Hu-man
Tell-ing
Prais-ing
Pray-ing,
What we

longed to know the way,
mas-ter, but as friend,
need to sat-is-fy,
of the Fa-ther's care,
Is-rael's sav-ing King,
"Fa-ther, use your Son,"
cel-e-brate is real;

Christ pro-claimed a ho-ly
Christ por-trayed the way of
Christ made e-ven trai-tors
Christ poured out him-self in
Hearts and voic-es made one
Christ a-lone could know its
Still Christ wel-comes to his

mys-t'ry;
serv-ice;
wel-come;
prom-ise;
mu-sic;
mean-ing;
ta-ble;

Still his words call us to-day.
Still in serv-ing we must bend.
Still we ques-tion, "Is it I?"
Still that cov'-nant we must share.
Still de-liv'r-ing love we sing.
Still we pray, "God's will be done."
Still Christ serves us at his meal.

Text: Paul A. Richardson, b.1951, © 1990, The Hymn Society. Administered by Hope Publishing Co.
Tune: OMNI DIE, 8 7 8 7; Corner's *Cross Catholisch Gesangbuch*, 1631; arr. William Smith Rockstro, 1895

1. See Mar - y set - ting out at dawn For Zi - on
2. There faith - ful Mar - y, meek, de - mure, Has come to
3. When Mar - y brings Mes - si - ah there, God an - swers
4. Be - cause she brings the Sav - ior there, Grey An - na
5. All have some spe - cial part to play In God's e -

with her six - week Son, And Jo - seph, tur - tle -
be ac - knowl - edged pure, Then ded - i - cates the
Sim - eon's life - long prayer For peace for him and
has a Gift to share. Had she not prayed, "Your
ter - nal plan who pray, "In heav'n, so here Your

doves in hand, To car - ry out the Lord's com - mand.
Ho - ly One By whom God's per - fect will is done.
ev - 'ry - one Who prays in faith, "Your will be done."
will be done," Who would have met and known God's Son?
will be done" At ev - 'ry ris - ing of the sun.

Text: Jaroslav J. Vajda, b.1919, © 1991, Concordia Publishing House
Tune: PUER NOBIS, LM; adapt. by Michael Praetorius, 1571-1621

122 This Is My Will

1. This is my will, my one com-mand, That love should
2. No great - er love can be than this: To choose to
3. I call you now no long - er slaves; No slave knows
4. You chose not me, but I chose you, That you should
5. All that you ask my Fa - ther dear For my name's

dwell a - mong you all. This is my will, that
die to save one's friends. You are my friends if
all his mas - ter does. I call you friends, for
go and bear much fruit. I chose you out that
sake you shall re - ceive. This is my will, my

you should love As I have shown that I love you.
you o - bey What I com-mand that you should do.
all I hear My Fa - ther say you hear from me.
you in me Should bear much fruit that will a - bide.
one com-mand, That love should dwell in each, in all.

Text: James Quinn, SJ, © 1994. Used by permission of Selah Publishing Co., Inc.
Tune: PUER NOBIS, LM; adapt. by Michael Praetorius, 1571-1621

1. No sign to us you give That eye can plain-ly see. Be-yond our bounds of sense you live In deep-est mys-ter-y.
2. No proof can clear the mind Or rid the heart of doubt. Though long we search, we can-not find Your truth with-in, with-out.
3. But o-ver ways un-trod In search of us you came. You turned to us a hu-man face And bore a hu-man name.
4. Lord, touch our eyes, still blind, With faith, trans-cend-ing sight, And show us truth we can-not find A-part from you, the Light.
5. Un-veil the truth con-cealed With-in the mys-ter-y Of love up-on a cross re-vealed For all hu-man-i-ty.

Text: Herman G. Stuempfle, b.1923, © 1997, GIA Publications, Inc.
Tune: SOUTHWELL, SM; Daman's *Psalmes*, 1579, alt.

124 Would I Have Answered when You Called

1. Would I have an - swered when you called, "Come,
2. Would I have fol - lowed where you led Through
3. Would I have matched my step with yours When
4. O Christ, I can - not search my heart Through

fol - low, fol - low me!"? Would I at once have
an - cient Gal - i - lee, On roads un - known, by
crowds cried, "Cru - ci - fy!", When on a rock - y
all its tan - gled ways, Nor can I with a

left be - hind Both work and fam - i - ly? Or
ways un - tried, Be - yond se - cu - ri - ty? Or
hill I saw A cross a - gainst the sky? Or
cer - tain mind My stead - fast - ness ap - praise. I

would the old, fa - mil - iar round Have
would I soon have hur - ried back Where
would I too have slipped a - way And
on - ly pray that when you call, "Come,

held me by its claim And kept the spark with -
home and com-fort drew, Where truth you taught would
left you there a - lone, A dy - ing king with
fol - low, fol - low me!", You'll give me strength be -

in my heart From burst - ing in - to flame?
not dis - turb The or - dered world I knew?
crown of thorns Up - on a ter - r'ble throne?
yond my own To fol - low faith - ful - ly.

Text: Herman G. Stuempfle, b.1923, © 1997, GIA Publications, Inc.
Tune: KINGSFOLD, CMD; English; harm. by Ralph Vaughan Williams, 1872-1958, © Oxford University Press, Inc.

125 Lord, Whose Love in Humble Service

1. Lord, whose love in hum-ble serv - ice Bore the weight of hu - man need, Who did on the Cross for - sak - en, Show us mer - cy's per - fect deed; We, your ser - vants, bring the wor - ship Not of
2. Still your chil - dren wan-der home - less; Still the hun - gry cry for bread; Still the cap - tives long for free - dom; Still in grief we mourn our dead. As, O Lord, your deep com - pas - sion Healed the
3. As we wor - ship, grant us vi - sion, Till your love's re - veal - ing light, Till the height and depth and great-ness Dawns up - on our hu - man sight: Mak - ing known the needs and bur - dens Your com -
4. Called from wor - ship in - to serv - ice Forth in your great name we go, To the child, the youth, the a - ged, Love in liv - ing deeds to show; Hope and health, good - will and com - fort, Coun - sel,

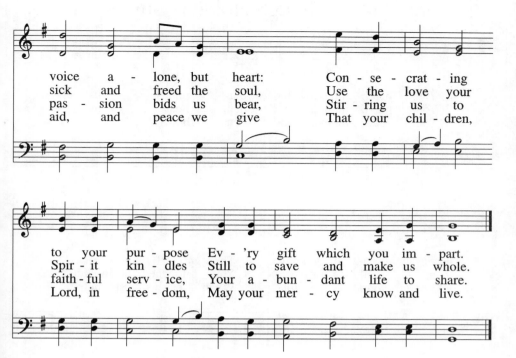

voice a - lone, but heart: Con - se - crat - ing
sick and freed the soul, Use the love your
pas - sion bids us bear, Stir - ring us to
aid, and peace we give That your chil - dren,

to your pur - pose Ev - 'ry gift which you im - part.
Spir - it kin - dles Still to save and make us whole.
faith - ful serv - ice, Your a - bun - dant life to share.
Lord, in free - dom, May your mer - cy know and live.

Text: Albert J. Bayly, 1901-1984, © Oxford University Press, Inc.
Tune: BEACH SPRING, 8 7 8 7 D; *The Sacred Harp*, 1844; harm. by Ronald A. Nelson, © 1978, *Lutheran Book of Worship*

126 Your Hand, Though Hidden, Guides Us

1. Your hand, though hid - den, guides us By
2. Your hand, though hid - den, heals us As
3. Your hand, though hid - den, holds us When

ways un - seen, un - known, Through all our rest - less
then, in Gal - i - lee, You touched the bound, the
all sup - port is gone, When earth's best help is

search - ing On paths we think our own.
bur - dened With grace that set them free.
fu - tile And hu - man strength un - done.

With si - lent step you has - ten To
Come now, O Lord, with heal - ing For
Then, though the night close round us And

meet us where we stray. Then pa - tient - ly you
grief and pain and sin. Come, touch our lives with
wind and wave as - sail, You grasp us in the

lead us A - long our pil - grim way.
mer - cy And make us whole a - gain.
dark - ness With love that does not fail.

Text: Herman G. Stuempfle, b.1923, © 1997, GIA Publications, Inc.
Tune: ST. THEODULPH, 7 6 7 6 D; Melchior Teschner, 1584-1635

127 Sleepers, Wake

1. "Sleep - ers, wake!" A voice a - stounds us, The
2. Zi - on hears the watch - men sing - ing; Her
3. Lamb of God, the heav'ns a - dore you; Let

shout of ram - part - guards sur - rounds us: "A -
heart with joy - ful hope is spring - ing, She
saints and an - gels sing be - fore you, As

wake, Je - ru - sa - lem, a - rise!" Mid - night's peace their
wakes and hur - ries through the night. Forth he comes, her
harps and cym - bals swell the sound. Twelve great pearls, the

cry has bro - ken, Their ur - gent sum - mons
Bride - groom glo - rious In strength of grace, in
cit - y's por - tals: Through them we stream to

clear-ly spo - ken: "The time has come, O maid - ens wise!
truth vic - to - rious: Her star is ris'n, her light grows bright.
join th' im-mor - tals As we with joy your throne sur - round.

Rise up, and give us light; The Bride-groom is in
Now come, most wor - thy Lord, God's Son, In - car - nate
No eye has known the sight, No ear heard such de -

sight. Al - le - lu - ia! Your lamps pre - pare And
Word, Al - le - lu - ia! We fol - low all And
light: Al - le - lu - ia! There - fore we sing To

has - ten there, That you the wed-ding feast may share."
heed your call To come in - to the ban - quet hall.
greet our King; For ev - er let our prais - es ring.

Text: Carl P. Daw, Jr., b.1944, © 1982, Hope Publishing Co.
Tune: WACHET AUF, 89 8 89 8 66 4 88; Philipp Nicolai, 1556-1608; harm. by J. S. Bach, 1685-1750

128　We Give God Thanks for Those Who Knew

1. We give God thanks for those who knew
The touch of Jesus' heal-ing love;
They trust-ed him to make them whole,
To give them peace, their guilt re-move.

2. We of-fer prayer for all who go
Re-ly-ing on God's grace and pow'r,
To help the anx-ious and the ill,
To heal their wounds, their lives re-store.

3. We ded-i-cate our skills and time
To those who suf-fer where we live,
To bring such com-fort as we can,
To meet their need, their pain re-lieve.

4. So, Je-sus' touch of heal-ing grace
Lives on with-in our will-ing care;
By thought and prayer and gifts we prove
His mer-cy still, his love we share.

Text: Michael Perry, b.1942, © 1982, Jubilate Hymns Ltd. Administered by Hope Publishing Co.
Tune: O WALY WALY, 8 8 8 8; English traditional; arr. by John L. Bell, b.1949, © 1989, Iona Community, GIA Publications, Inc., agent

O Risen Christ, You Search Our Hearts   129

1. O Ris - en Christ, you search our hearts With
2. "Yes, Lord, we love you!" we pro - test. "Have
3. "Friend, do you love me more than these— Than
4. "Yes, Lord, we love you," we re - ply, "Be -
5. Christ, help us live the love we speak, Our

love's all see - ing eye And ask us, "Do you
you not heard our praise, Nor seen that we have
com - fort, praise, and wealth? And do you love me
yond all oth - er good; But tempt - ed, test - ed,
sa - cred vows to keep, To hear and an - swer

love me most?" And wait for our re - ply.
fol - lowed you And served you all our days?"
more than this— Your close - ly guard - ed self?"
still we fail To serve you as we should."
when you call, "Now go, and feed my sheep!"

Text: Herman G. Stuempfle, b.1923, © 2000, GIA Publications, Inc.
Tune: LAND OF REST, CM; American; harm. by Annabel M. Buchanan, 1888-1983, © 1938, J. Fisher and Bro.

130 May God's Love Be Fixed Above You

1. May God's love be fixed a-bove you, O - ver-
2. May God's love ad - vance be - fore you, Vig - i -
3. May God's love be close be - side you, Qual - i -
4. May God's love re - main up - on you, And, your

shad - ow you with grace; May God's love stand firm be -
lant of all your ways; May God's love keep watch be -
fy you for life's race; May God's love live deep with -
faith - ful - ness re - pay, With a peace the world can't

neath you, Wel - come you with glad em - brace. Al - le - lu - ia!
hind you, Shield - ing you through all your days. Al - le - lu - ia!
in you, With as - sur - ance, last - ing grace. Al - le - lu - ia!
give you, Nei - ther shall it take a - way. Al - le - lu - ia!

Al - le - lu - ia! Glo - ri - fy the Lord with praise!
Al - le - lu - ia! Glo - ri - fy the Lord with praise!
Al - le - lu - ia! Glo - ri - fy the Lord with praise!
Al - le - lu - ia! Glo - ri - fy the Lord this day!

Text: John A. Dalles, © 2000, GIA Publications, Inc.
Tune: LAUDA ANIMA, 8 7 8 7 8 7; John Goss, 1800-1880

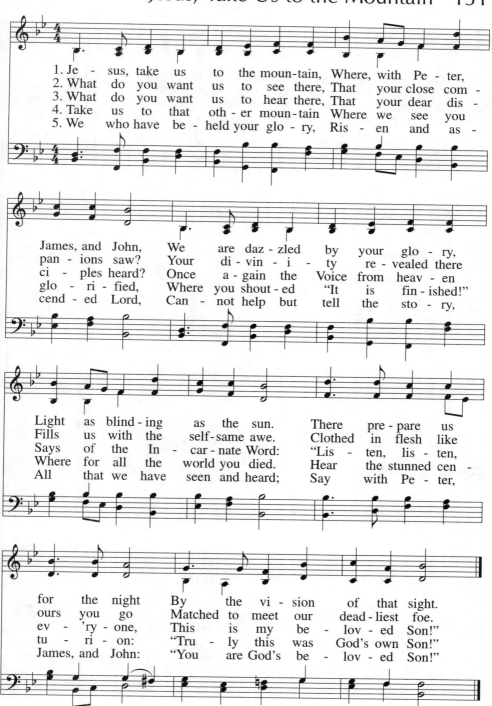

1. Je - sus, take us to the moun-tain, Where, with Pe - ter,
2. What do you want us to see there, That your close com -
3. What do you want us to hear there, That your dear dis -
4. Take us to that oth - er moun-tain Where we see you
5. We who have be - held your glo - ry, Ris - en and as -

James, and John, We are daz - zled by your glo - ry,
pan - ions saw? Your di - vin - i - ty re - vealed there
ci - ples heard? Once a - gain the Voice from heav - en
glo - ri - fied, Where you shout - ed "It is fin - ished!"
cend - ed Lord, Can - not help but tell the sto - ry,

Light as blind - ing as the sun. There pre - pare us
Fills us with the self-same awe. Clothed in flesh like
Says of the In - car - nate Word: "Lis - ten, lis - ten,
Where for all the world you died. Hear the stunned cen -
All that we have seen and heard; Say with Pe - ter,

for the night By the vi - sion of that sight.
ours you go Matched to meet our dead - liest foe.
ev - 'ry - one, This is my be - lov - ed Son!"
tu - ri - on: "Tru - ly this was God's own Son!"
James, and John: "You are God's be - lov - ed Son!"

Text: Jaroslav J. Vajda, b.1919, © 1991, Concordia Publishing House
Tune: UNSER HERRSCHER, 8 7 8 7 77; Joachim Neander, 1650-1680

132 The Virtue of Humility

1. The virtue of humility Revokes the law of gravity, Makes low be high and high be low, Turns upside-down the world we know.
2. On virtue's ladder, Gospel friend, By climbing downward we ascend; By counting all our gain as loss, We come to glory in the cross.
3. How quick are we to covet fame And draw the glory to our name? But Jesus gives the acid test: "The great among you serve the rest."
4. Accepting our humanity, Ascending by humility, From Jesus let us learn the art Of serving God with humble heart.

Text: Delores Dufner, OSB, © 1995, 1996, Sisters of St. Benedict
Tune: PUER NOBIS, LM; adapt. by Michael Praetorius, 1571-1621

133 Blessed Jesus, Living Bread

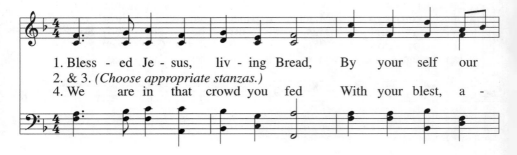

1. Blessed Jesus, living Bread, By yourself our
2. & 3. *(Choose appropriate stanzas.)*
4. We are in that crowd you fed With your blest, a-

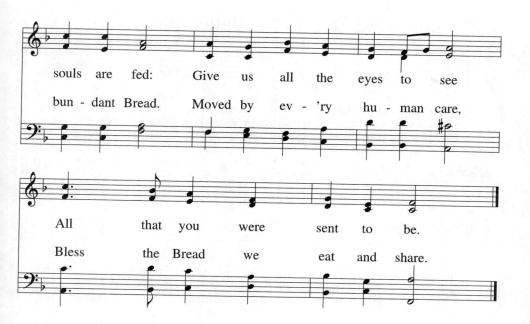

souls are fed: Give us all the eyes to see
bun - dant Bread. Moved by ev - 'ry hu - man care,

All that you were sent to be.
Bless the Bread we eat and share.

A. Stanzas 2 & 3 for John 6:1-15 (Pentecost 10)

2. "What is it" old Israel cried,
   ate it and were satisfied.
   Now the same prolific hand
   feeds them in a barren land.

3. "Who is it?" who gives himself
   bread-like from a baker's shelf?
   Never-ending food supply:
   those who eat it never die.

B. Stanzas 2 & 3 for John 6:24-35

2. To the House of Bread you came,
   there received your saving Name
   from that lowly manger bed
   all the dying world is fed.

3. Not by this world's bread alone
   Can our life become full-grown,
   But by every word that goes
   From the mouth of God—one grows.

C. Stanzas 2 & 3 for John 6:41-51

2. Word of God by which we live:
   What we hunger for you give—
   For the body and the soul,
   Life with God, life new and whole.

3. All we ever need and more,
   Flowing from your boundless store;
   At your table every guest
   Sees your mercy manifest.

D. Stanzas 2 & 3 for John 6:51-58

2. No more perfect food is there
   Than the food you came to share,
   Not to be admired alone,
   Lest one spurn it for a stone.

3. On that table made of wood
   Lies our sacramental food:
   "Take and eat and live" you call,
   "Here is life for each and all!"

E. Stanzas 2 & 3 for John 6:60-67

2. Ah, what welcome words you speak:
   Comfort to revive the weak,
   God's own wisdom, hope, and cheer
   Starving souls are blest to hear.

3. Word Incarnate, Word divine
   Word that comes in bread and wine:
   Love that we have come to know:
   Lord, to whom else shall we go?

Text: Jaroslav Vajda, b.1919, ©1990, Concordia Publishing House
Tune: ORIENTIS PARTIBUS, 7 7 7 7; French Melody, 13th c. attr. Pierre de Corbeil; harm. Richard Redhead, 1853.

134 Salvation! There's No Better Word

1. Sal - va - tion! there's no bet - ter word For what Christ does for
2. Sal - va - tion! there's no bet - ter word For what Christ of - fers
3. Sal - va - tion! there's no bet - ter word For all Christ came to

me: He saves me from re - pent - ed sins And
us— The love that died for you and me Up -
do: His peace re - moves the bar - ri - cades And

sets my spir - it free. O save me ab - so -
on a Ro - man cross. As ser - vants of your
lets for - give - ness through. O fill your u - ni -

lute - ly, Lord, That I may play my part As
King - dom, Lord, O nev - er let us rest Un -
ver - sal Church With wis - dom, Lord, and love; And

your dis - ci - ple, dai - ly more Ma - ture in mind and heart!
til your love and jus - tice reach The need - y and op-pressed!
save this pow - er - hun - gry world With pow-er from a - bove!

Text: Fred Pratt Green, 1903-2000, © 1974, Hope Publishing Co.
Tune: ELLACOMBE, CMD; *Gesangbuch der Herzogl*, Wirtemberg, 1784

We Need No Ladder Now   135

1. We need no lad - der now To
2. You come to us to - day, As
3. You seek us, God of grace, While
4. We need no lad - der now. By

reach your throne, O God. You clothed your Word in
then in Gal - i - lee, To show in Christ your
we are still a - far And, with a love be -
faith you help us see The Christ in whom you

hu - man flesh; Our com - mon earth you trod.
hid - den face That eyes still blind may see.
yond our dreams, Em - brace us where we are.
touched our earth With your e - ter - ni - ty.

Text: Herman G. Stuempfle, b.1923, © 1997, GIA Publications, Inc.
Tune: POTSDAM, SM; J.S. Bach, 1685-1750, adapt.

136 Sovereign Maker of All Things

1. Sov - 'reign Mak - er of all things, God of cov - e - nant and grace, Ev - 'ry crea - ture knows your pow'r, Quakes with fear be - fore your face. But your mer - cy far ex - ceeds What our minds can com - pre - hend;

2. You have prom - ised to for - give Con - trite sin - ners who re - pent; So I come with hum - bled heart, By your word made con - fi - dent. I have sinned, Lord, I have sinned: Well I know my wick - ed - ness.

3. Let me not be lost in sin, Ban - ished to e - ter - nal night; God who hears the pen - i - tent, Let your good - ness show your might. Though I be un - wor - thy, Lord, Your great mer - cy will I claim,

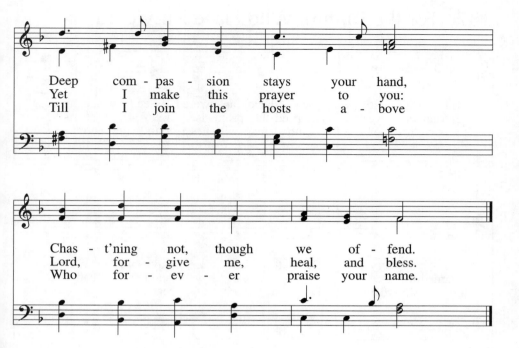

Deep   com - pas - sion   stays   your   hand,
Yet   I   make   this   prayer   to   you:
Till   I   join   the   hosts   a - bove

Chas - t'ning   not,   though   we   of - fend.
Lord,   for - give   me,   heal,   and   bless.
Who   for - ev - er   praise   your   name.

Text: Carl P. Daw, Jr., b.1945, © 1990, Hope Publishing Co.
Tune: ST. GEORGE'S WINDSOR, 7 7 7 7 D; George J. Elvey, 1816-1893

137 For the Faithful Who Have Answered

1. For the faith-ful who have an-swered When they heard your
2. Man-y eyes have glimpsed the prom-ise. Man-y hearts have
3. For this cloud of faith-ful wit-ness, For the com-mon

call to serve, For the man-y ways you led them
yearned to see. Man-y ears have heard you call-ing
life we share, For the work of peace and jus-tice,

Test-ing will and stretch-ing nerve, For their work and
Us to great-er lib-er-ty. Some have fal-len
For the gos-pel that we bear, For the vi-sion

for their wit-ness As they strove a-gainst the odds,
in the strug-gle. Oth-ers still are fight-ing on.
that our home-land Is your love— deep, high and broad—

For their cour - age and o - be - dience
You are not a - shamed to own us.
For the dif - f'rent roads we trav - el

We give thanks and praise, O God.
We give thanks and praise, O God.
We give thanks and praise, O God.

Text: Sylvia Dunstan, 1955-1993, © 1991, GIA Publications, Inc.
Tune: OMNE DIE, 8 7 8 7 D; *Trier Gesangbuch*, 1695

138 Christ, Your Footprints through the Desert

1. Christ, your foot - prints through the des - ert
2. Christ, you heard the stir - ring sum - mons
3. Son of God, the road from Jor - dan
4. God, in bap - tism you have made us

Led to Jor - dan's flow - ing stream.
As by Jor - dan's bank you stood;
Led at last to Cal - v'ry's hill.
One with Christ, our ris - en Lord;

There you heard the her - ald cry - ing
Bathed, though sin - less, with your peo - ple
There up - on the cross for - sak - en,
Freed us, claimed us, cleansed, for - giv - en

Is - rael's old, pro - phet - ic dream:
In the riv - er's cleans - ing flood.
You ful - filled the Fa - ther's will.
Through the wa - ter and the Word.

"He   is   com - ing!   He   is   com - ing!
High   a - bove,   the   heav - ens   o - pened;
Lamb   of   God,   we   see   you   dy - ing,
Help   us   hear   your   ur - gent   sum - mons,

He   will   cleanse   the   earth   with   flame!
Came   the   Spir - it   as   a   dove;
Sin - less,   yet   for   sin - ners   slain.
Call - ing   us   to   serve   you   now.

Sin - ners,   plunge   be - neath   the   wa - ters!
Spoke   a   Voice   be - yond   all   hear - ing:
But   where   death   rose   up   to   tri - umph,
Send   us   forth,   your   sons   and   daugh - ters,

Wash   a - way   your   guilt   and   shame!"
"See   my   Son,   the   One   I   love!"
You   be - gan   your   glo - rious   reign!
With   the   cross   up - on   our   brow.

Text: Herman G. Stuempfle, b.1923, © 2000, GIA Publications, Inc.
Tune: EBENEZER, 8 7 8 7 D; Thomas J. Williams, 1869-1944

139 Lone He Prays Within the Garden

unison

1. Lone he prays with - in the Gar - den
2. Lone he stands in Pi - late's court - room,
3. Lone he hangs up - on a hill - top
4. Christ is ris - en in the gar - den

Where dis - ci - ples, sleep - ing, lie.
Judge of all the na - tions, judged.
Un - der - neath a sun - less sky,
Where, en - tombed, he lay a - lone.

None to share his grief and tor - ment;
Friends have fled, be - trayed, for - sak - en;
Cries to God but hears no an - swer;
Chris - tians, run with joy to greet him,

None   to   hear   his   an - guished   cry.
Sol - diers   bound   him,   mocked   and   scourged.
None   but   scof - fers   make   re - ply.
Shin - ing   bright - er   than   the   sun!

Does   the   God   who   hides   in   dark - ness
Will   the   God   who   guards   the   right - eous
Is   the   Son   by   God   for - sak - en,
Chris - tians,   nev - er   doubt   the   prom - ise:

Will   his   on - ly   Son   to   die?
Watch   while   e - vil   reigns,   un - purged?
Left   up - on   a   Cross   to   die?
God   does   not   for - sake   his   own!

Text: Herman G. Stuempfle, b.1923, © 1993, GIA Publications, Inc.
Tune: PICARDY, 8 7 8 7 8 7; French Carol; harm. by Richard Proulx, b.1937, © 1986, GIA Publications, Inc.

140 To Love Just Those Who Love You

1. To love just those who love you Is
2. To laugh just with those who please you And
3. Since Christ is Truth and Teach - er, The

rare - ly hard to do, For e - ven un - be -
share a sim - ple joy Is dif - f'rent from en -
Day Star and the Day, The Life and our Life -

liev - ers Love those who love them
dur - ing The peo - ple who an -
giv - er, Way - far - er and the

too. But you must love, said Je - sus, Those
noy; And those you hate, said Je - sus, Or
Way, If you would come, said Je - sus, And

you don't care a - bout, And feed them if they're
wound you deep with - in, Are still your Fa - ther's
my com - pan - ion be, In love and joy and

hun - gry Though you then go with - out.
chil - dren And must be claimed as kin.
suf - f'ring You'll walk God's path with me.

Text: Rae E. Whitney, © 1995, Selah Publishing Co., Inc.
Tune: PASSION CHORALE, 7 6 7 6 D; Hans Leo Hassler, 1564-1612; harm. by J. S. Bach, 1685-1750

141 Mark How the Lamb of God's Self-Offering

1. Mark how the Lamb of God's self - of - f'ring
2. From this as - sur - ance of God's fa - vor
3. Grant us, O God, the strength and cour - age

Our hu - man sin - ful - ness takes on
Je - sus goes to the wil - der - ness,
To live the faith our lips de - clare;

In the birth - wa - ters of the Jor - dan
There to en - dure a time of test - ing
Bless us in our bap - tis - mal call - ing;

As Je - sus is bap - tized by John.
That read - ied him to teach and bless.
Christ's roy - al priest - hood help us share.

Hear how the voice from heav - en thun - ders,
So we, by wa - ter and the Spir - it
Turn us from ev - 'ry false al - le - giance,

"Lo, this is my be - lov - ed Son."
Bap - tized in - to Christ's min - is - try,
That we may trust in Christ a - lone:

See how in dove - like form the Spir - it
Are of - ten led to paths of serv - ice
Raise up in us a cho - sen peo - ple

De - scends on God's A - noint - ed One.
Through maz - es of ad - ver - si - ty.
Trans - formed by love to be your own.

Text: Carl P. Daw, Jr., b.1944, © 1990, Hope Publishing Co.
Tune: RENDEZ À DIEU, 9 8 9 8 D; Louis Bourgeois, c.1510-1561

142 Lord, Grant Us Grace to Know the Time

1. Lord, grant us grace to know the time Of
2. We seek your Word, as Mar - y sought; We
3. Your Word a - lone gives need - ed pow'r To
4. But you have taught that love is feigned That
5. We thank you, Lord, for qui - et time To

ac - tion or of prayer, Which hour to crowd with
wait in qui - et - ness, And yet we ask for
strength - en wea - ry hands And helps us see in
fails a neigh - bor's need, That faith we claim is
cast our care on you And for your Word that

wait - ing work And which with you to share.
strength to serve With Mar - tha's faith - ful - ness.
each new day The way of your com - mands.
false un - til Your Word be - comes our deed.
fol - lows us When work be - comes our prayer.

Text: Herman G. Stuempfle, b.1923, © 1997, GIA Publications, Inc.
Tune: ST. ANNE, CM; attr. to William Croft, 1678-1727; harm. composite from 18th c. versions

1. A - lone and filled with fear,
2. We dare to ques - tion you,
3. You probe our deep - est need,
4. The Word you speak is filled
5. But born a - new by love,
6. All glo - ry be to God

We
As
Our
With
The
Who

come to you by night, Our trou - bled, rest - less
though all truth we knew, But find you are the
hid - den fears ad - dress. You lead us to the
prom - ise and with pain: "There is no eas - y
old life left be - hind, We pass from dark - ness
sent to us the Son, Who will not give our

spir - its drawn To you, the Light from Light.
Ques - tion - er Who knows us through and through.
mid - night hour Where we, un - masked, con - fess.
road to life; You must be born a - gain!"
in - to day And life, long sought, we find.
spir - its rest Till love's great work is done.

Text: Herman G. Stuempfle, b.1923, © 1997, GIA Publications, Inc.
Tune: FRANCONIA, SM; Johann b. Konig, 1691-1758; adapt. by William H. Havergal

144 When to Mary, the Word

1. When to Mar - y, the Word, From the throne of the
2. At the sound of her voice, Did her cous - in re -
3. Like our Moth - er, we should Give our neigh - bor our
4. And as John sure-ly knew, Al - though hid - den from

Lord, Made the jour - ney to earth on that day,
joice, While the babe in her womb danced a - round,
good, As with - in us the se - cret is hid;
view, That the Lord was in - deed with them there,

Mar - y turned not with - in, But with haste, to her kin
For when Je - sus, the Lamb, Spoke his si - lent, "I am,"
For, in truth, then will show For all oth - ers to know
So may we, with de - light, Take with - in our own sight

She set out for a land far a - way.
Proph-et's ears filled with joy at the sound.
All the won - ders that God for us did.
Je - sus liv - ing in souls ev - 'ry - where.

Text: Patricia Blaze Clark, © 1998, GIA Publications, Inc.
Tune: MIDDLEBURY, 66 9 66 9, *Southern Harmony*, 1835; harm. by Jack W. Burnam, b.1946, © 1984

1. A sow-er's seed fell on a path Packed hard by foot and cart, And hun-gry spar-rows ate their fill Be-fore a root could start. Lord,
2. And some fell down where rock-y ground No sus-te-nance could give. Be-neath the scorch-ing noon-day sun No ten-der plant could live. Lord,
3. And some seed fell a-mong the weeds That wove a tan-gling snare To choke the green and bud-ding plants That nev-er fruit would bear. Lord,
4. But some seed fell on fer-tile soil And flour-ished more and more Un-til the joy-ous har-vest time, When hun-dred-fold it bore. Lord,

give us ears to hear your Word And hearts where seed can grow.

Text: Herman G. Stuempfle, b.1923, © 2000, GIA Publications, Inc.
Tune: MORNING SONG, 8 6 8 6 8 6; Wyeth's *Repository of Sacred Music*, 1813; harm. by C. Winfred Douglas, 1867-1944

146 They Came, a Milling Crowd

1. They came, a mill - ing crowd, And
2. And then, when eve - ning came, They
3. How great the mys - ter - y! The
4. Once more, O Christ, we come, A
5. All praise to you, O Christ, By

gath - ered round the Lord. He loved them with a
hun - gered and were fed From of - fered loaves he
loaves were mul - ti - plied, And still we feed up -
rest - less, hun - g'ring throng To hear your Word and
whom we now are fed. Our Host, a - gain you

shep - herd's heart And fed them with his Word.
blessed and broke And made their liv - ing bread.
on the crumbs And still are sat - is - fied!
taste your bread And sing sal - va - tion's song.
share with us Your - self, the liv - ing bread.

Text: Herman G. Stuempfle, b.1923, © 1993, GIA Publications, Inc.
Tune: FRANCONIA, SM; Johann b. Konig, 1691-1758; adapt. by William H. Havergal

1. Be - fore the fruit is rip - ened by the sun,
2. Be - fore the East - er Al - le - lu - ias ring,
3. Be - fore we gain the grace that comes through loss,

Be - fore the pet - als or the leaves un - coil,
Be - fore the mas - sive rock is rolled a - side,
Be - fore we live by more than bread and breath,

Be - fore the first fine silk - en root is spun,
Be - fore the fear of death has lost its sting,
Be - fore we lift in joy an emp - ty cross,

A seed is dropped and bur - ied in the soil.
A just and lov - ing man is cru - ci - fied.
We face with Christ the seed's re - new - ing death.

Text: Thomas H. Troeger, b.1945, © 1985, Oxford University Press, Inc.
Tune: SURSUM CORDA, 10 10 10 10; Alfred M. Smith, 1879-1971, © Mrs. Alfred M. Smith

148 When Jesus Walked beside the Shore

1. When Je - sus walked be - side the shore Of
2. "Launch out a - gain up - on the sea!" His
3. Then Pe - ter fell up - on his knees And
4. O Mas - ter, as by Gal - i - lee You

an - cient Gal - i - lee, Four fish - er - men were
words were firm and plain. "But, Lord, in vain we've
cried, "De - part from me! How can a sin - ner
called those four a - side And, when they launched up -

mend - ing nets They'd cast up - on the sea.
toiled the night; Why should we try a - gain?"
such as I Be - hold such maj - es - ty?"
on the deep Their la - bors mul - ti - plied:

All night they fished, but emp - ty nets Were
In spite of doubt, they set their sails And
But Je - sus raised him up a - gain And
So come to us and call us forth To

all they pulled on board; And emp - ty hopes were
cast their nets once more; And such a catch they
an a - pos - tle made: "For peo - ple now you'll
ven - tures in your name, And help us, leav - ing

all they had Un - til they met the Lord.
brought a - board They scarce could reach the shore.
cast your net; You must not be a - fraid!"
fear be - hind, Your king - dom's truth pro - claim.

Text: Herman G. Stuempfle, © 1993, GIA Publications, Inc.
Tune: FOREST GREEN, CMD; English; harm. by Ralph Vaughan Williams, 1872-1958, © Oxford University Press, Inc.

149 Transform Us As You, Transfigured

unison

1. Trans - form us as you, trans - fig - ured,
2. Trans - form us as you, trans - fig - ured,
3. Trans - form us as you, trans - fig - ured,

Stood a - part on Ta - bor's height.
Once spoke with those ho - ly ones.
Would not stay with - in a shrine.

Lead us up our sa - cred moun - tains,
We, sur - round - ed by the wit - ness
Keep us from our great temp - ta - tion—

Search us with re - veal - ing light.
Of those saints whose work is done,
Time and truth we quick - ly bind,

Lift   us   from where we   have   fall -   en,
Live   in   this world as   your   Bod -   y,
Lead   us   down those dai   -   ly   path -   ways

Full   of   ques - tions,   filled   with   fright.
Cho -   sen   daugh - ters,   cho   -   sen   sons.
Where   our   love   is   not   -   con   -   fined.

Text: Sylvia Dunstan, 1955-1993, © 1993, GIA Publications, Inc.
Tune: PICARDY, 8 7 8 7 8 7; French Carol; harm. by Richard Proulx, b.1937, © 1986, GIA Publications, Inc.

150 Lord, Help Us Walk Your Servant Way

1. Lord, help us walk your ser - vant way Wher -
2. You came to earth, O Christ, as Lord, But
3. No gold - en scep - ter but a towel You
4. You bid us bend our hu - man pride Nor
5. Lord, help us walk your ser - vant way Wher -

ev - er love may lead And, bend - ing low, for -
pow'r you laid a - side. You lived your years in
place with - in the hands Of those who seek to
count our - selves a - bove The low - est place, the
ev - er love may lead And bend - ing low, for -

get - ting self, Each serve the oth - er's need.
ser - vant - hood, In low - li - ness you died.
fol - low you And live by your com - mands.
mean - est task That waits the gift of love.
get - ting self, Each serve the oth - er's need.

Text: Herman G. Stuempfle, b.1923, © 1997, GIA Publications, Inc.
Tune: ST. PETER, CM; Alexander Robert Reinagle

When Jesus Came to Jordan 151

1. When Je-sus came to Jor-dan To be bap-tised by John,
2. He came to share temp-ta-tion, Our ut-most woe and loss,
3. Come, Ho-ly Spir-it, aid us To keep the vows we make.

He did not come for par-don, But as his Fa-ther's Son.
For us and our sal-va-tion To die up-on the cross.
This ver-y day in-vade us, And ev-'ry bond-age break.

He came to share re-pen-tance With all who mourn their sins,
So when the Dove de-scend-ed On him, the Son of Man,
Come, give our lives di-rec-tion, The gift we cov-et most:

To speak the vi-tal sen-tence With which good news be-gins.
The hid-den years had end-ed, The age of grace be-gan.
To share the res-ur-rec-tion That leads to Pen-te-cost.

Text: Fred Pratt Green, 1903-2000, © 1980, Hope Publishing Co.
Tune: MERLE'S TUNE, 7 6 7 6 D; Hal H. Hopson, b.1933, © 1983, Hope Publishing Co.

152 Silence! Frenzied, Unclean Spirit

1. "Si - lence! Fren - zied, un - clean spir - it,"
2. Lord, the de - mons still are thriv - ing
3. Si - lence, Lord, the un - clean spir - it,

Cried God's heal - ing, ho - ly One.
In the grey cells of the mind:
In our mind and in our heart.

"Cease your rant - ing! Flesh can't bear it.
Ty - rant voic - es shrill and driv - ing,
Speak your word that when we hear it

Flee as night be - fore the sun."
Twist - ed thoughts that grip and bind,
All our de - mons shall de - part.

At Christ's voice the de - mon trem - bled,
Doubts that stir the heart to pan - ic,
Clear our thought and calm our feel - ing,

From its vic - tim mad - ly rushed,
Fears dis - tort - ing rea - son's sight,
Still the frac - tured, war - ring soul.

While the crowd that was as - sem - bled
Guilt that makes our lov - ing fran - tic,
By the pow - er of your heal - ing

Stood in won - der, stunned and hushed.
Dreams that cloud the soul with fright.
Make us faith - ful, true and whole.

Text: Thomas H. Troeger, b.1945, © 1994, Oxford University Press, Inc.
Tune: EBENEZER, 8 7 8 7 D; Thomas J. Williams, 1869-1944

153 This Is Your Coronation

1. This is your cor - o - na - tion; Thorns
2. E - ter - nal judge on tri - al, God's
3. High Priest, you are a - noint - ed With

pressed up - on your head. No bright an - gel - ic
law, by law de - nied, Love's jus - tice is re -
blood up - on your face. And in this hour ap -

her - alds, But an - gry crowds in -
ject - ed And truth is fal - si -
point - ed The of - f'ring for our

stead. Be - neath your throne of tim - ber, And
fied. We who have charged, con - demned you Are
race. For weak - ness in - ter - ced - ing, For

strug - gling with the load. You go in cruel pro -
sen - tenced by your love. Your blood pro - nounc - es
sin, you are the price, For us your prayer un -

ces - sion On sor - row's roy - al road.
par - don As you are stretched a - bove.
ceas - ing O liv - ing sac - ri - fice.

Text: Sylvia Dunstan, 1955-1993, © 1995, GIA Publications, Inc.
Tune: PASSION CHORALE, 7 6 7 6 D; Hans Leo Hassler, 1564-1612; harm. by J. S. Bach, 1685-1750

154 The Temple Rang with Golden Coins

1. The tem-ple rang with gold-en coins The
2. A wid-ow came with cop-per coins And
3. When Je-sus saw her cost-ly gift And
4. At last he brought his of-fer-ing And
5. Lord, help us all, with you, to yield What

rich in bright ar - ray Con - trib-ut - ed from
of - fered them in praise. They were the last she
knew she had no more, He praised a love that
laid it on a tree; There gave him-self, his
ev - er love de - mands And free-ly give, as

gleam-ing hoards Their scales could scarce - ly weigh.
had to give Or save for dark - er days.
spared not self And called her rich, though poor.
life, his love For all hu - man - i - ty.
you have giv'n, With o - pen hearts and hands.

Text: Herman G. Stuempfle, b.1923, © 1993, GIA Publications, Inc.
Tune: AZMON, CM; Carl G. Gläser, 1784-1829; harm. by Lowell Mason, 1792-1872

God! When Human Bonds Are Broken 155

1. God! When hu - man bonds are bro - ken
2. Through that still - ness, with your Spir - it
3. You in us are bruised and bro - ken:
4. Send us, God of new be - gin - nings,
5. Give us faith to be more faith - ful,

And we lack the love or skill To re - store the
Come in - to our world of stress, For the sake of
Hear us as we seek re - lease From the pain of
Hum - bly hope - ful in - to life. Use us as a
Give us hope to be more true, Give us love to

hope of heal - ing, Give us grace and make us still.
Christ for - giv - ing All the fail - ures we con - fess.
ear - lier liv - ing: Set us free and grant us peace.
means of bless - ing: Make us stron - ger, give us faith.
go on learn - ing: God! En - cour - age and re - new!

Text: Fred Kaan, b.1929, © 1989, Hope Publishing Co.
Tune: STUTTGART, 8 7 8 7; *Psalmodia Sacra*, 1715; adapt. and harm. by William Henry Havergal, 1793-1870, alt.

156 For the Fruits of This Creation

1. For the fruits of this cre - a - tion, Thanks be to
2. In the just re - ward of la - bor, God's will is
3. For the har - vests of the Spir - it, Thanks be to

God; For these gifts to ev - 'ry na - tion,
done; In the help we give our neigh - bor,
God; For the good we all in - her - it,

Thanks be to God; For the plow - ing,
God's will is done; In our world - wide
Thanks be to God; For the won - ders

sow - ing, reap - ing, Si - lent growth while we are sleep - ing,
task of car - ing For the hun - gry and de - spair - ing,
that a - stound us, For the truths that still con - found us,

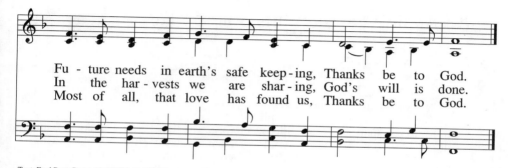

Fu - ture needs in earth's safe keep-ing, Thanks be to God.
In the har - vests we are shar-ing, God's will is done.
Most of all, that love has found us, Thanks be to God.

Text: Fred Pratt Green, 1903-2000, © 1970, Hope Publishing Co.
Tune: AR HYD Y NOS, 8 4 8 4 888 4; Welsh

The Thirsty Cry for Water, Lord 157

1. The thirst - y cry for wa - ter, Lord; The
2. The cup of wa - ter poured in love The
3. But help us al - so hear the cry Of
4. And come to us, O ris - en Christ, Our

hun - gry plead for bread. And man - y long
pangs of thirst will still. The bread of earth
hun - g'ring, thirst - ing hearts For liv - ing wa -
rest - less souls re - lieve; And sat - is - fy

to rise a - gain Where hope, cast down, lies dead.
you bid us share, The fam - ished child can fill.
ter, bread of life Your grace a - lone im - parts.
our starv - ing hearts That we may rise and live.

Text: Herman G. Stuempfle, b.1923, © 1997, GIA Publications, Inc.
Tune: NEW BRITAIN, CM; *Virginia Harmony*, 1831; harm. by Edwin O. Excell, 1851-1921

158 Again We Keep this Solemn Fast

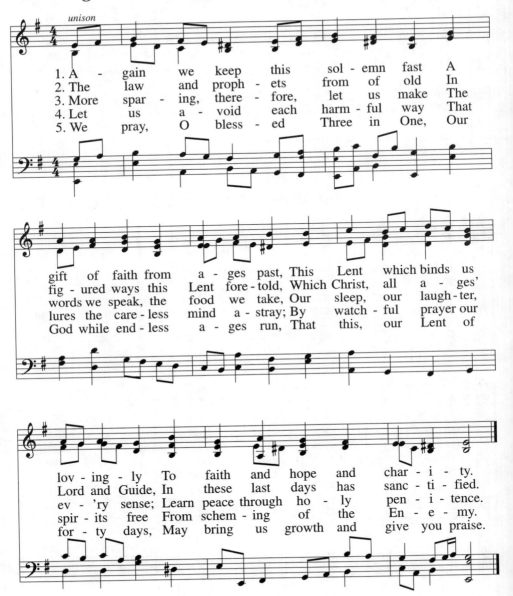

1. A - gain we keep this sol - emn fast A
   gift of faith from a - ges past, This Lent which binds us
   lov - ing - ly To faith and hope and char - i - ty.

2. The law and proph - ets from of old In
   fig - ured ways this Lent fore - told, Which Christ,
   all a - ges' Lord and Guide, In these last days has sanc - ti - fied.

3. More spar - ing, there - fore, let us make The
   words we speak, the food we take, Our sleep, our laugh - ter,
   ev - 'ry sense; Learn peace through ho - ly pen - i - tence.

4. Let us a - void each harm - ful way That
   lures the care - less mind a - stray; By watch - ful prayer our
   spir - its free From schem - ing of the En - e - my.

5. We pray, O bless - ed Three in One, Our
   God while end - less a - ges run, That this, our Lent of
   for - ty days, May bring us growth and give you praise.

Text: *Ex more docti mystico*; ascr. to Gregory the Great, c.540-604; tr. by Peter J. Scagnelli, b.1949, ©
Tune: ERHALT UNS HERR, LM; Klug's *Geistliche Lieder*, 1543; harm. by J.S. Bach, 1685-1750

The Church of Christ in Every Age   159

1. The Church of Christ in ev - 'ry age Be - set by change but Spir - it led, Must claim and test its her - it - age And keep on ris - ing from the dead.
2. A - cross the world, a - cross the street, The vic - tims of in - jus - tice cry For shel - ter and for bread to eat, And nev - er live un - til they die.
3. Then let the ser - vant Church a - rise, A car - ing Church that longs to be A part - ner in Christ's sac - ri - fice, And clothed in Christ's hu - man - i - ty.
4. For he a - lone, whose blood was shed, Can cure the fe - ver in our blood, And teach us how to share our bread And feed the starv - ing mul - ti - tude.
5. We have no mis - sion but to serve In full o - be - dience to our Lord: To care for all, with - out re - serve, And spread his lib - er - at - ing Word.

Text: Fred Pratt Green, 1903-2000, © 1971, Hope Publishing Co.
Tune: WAREHAM, LM; William Knapp, 1698-1768

Acknowledgments/*continued*

66 Text: © 2000, GIA Publications, Inc. Tune: From *The English Hymnal,* © Oxford University Press, Inc.

67 Text: © 1994, Selah Publishing Co., Inc., Kingston, NY 12401, www.selahpub.com. All rights reserved.

68 Text: © 2000, GIA Publications, Inc.

69 Text: © 1995, GIA Publications, Inc.

70 Text: © 1997, Hope Publishing Co., Carol Stream, IL 60188. All rights reserved. Used by permission. Tune: Harm. © 1978, *Lutheran Book of Worship.* Reprinted by permission of Augsburg Fortress

71 Text: © 1993, GIA Publications, Inc.

72 Text: © 1974, Hope Publishing Co., Carol Stream, IL 60188. All rights reserved. Used by permission. Tune: Harm. © 1938 (Renewed 1966) J. FISHER AND BRO. All Rights Assigned and Controlled by BELWIN-MILLS PUBLISHING CORP. (ASCAP) All Rights Reserved. Used by Permission.

73 Text: © 1988, The Pilgrim Press

74 Text: © 1997, GIA Publications, Inc. Tune: © 1983, Hope Publishing Co., Carol Stream, IL 60188. All rights reserved. Used by permission.

75 © 1996, Hope Publishing Co., Carol Stream, IL 60188. All rights reserved. Used by permission.

76 Text: © 1997, GIA Publications, Inc.

77 Text: © 1987, Hope Publishing Co., Carol Stream, IL 60188. All rights reserved. Used by permission.

78 Text: © 2000, GIA Publications, Inc. Tune: Harm. from *The English Hymnal,* © Oxford University Press, Inc.

79 Text: © 1987, Van Ness Press, Inc. All rights reserved. Used by permission. Tune: Harm. © 1978, *Lutheran Book of Worship.* Reprinted by permission of Augsburg Fortress

80 Text: From *The Incendiary Fellowship* by David Elton © 1967, David Elton Trueblood. Reprinted by permission of HarperCollins Publishers, Inc.

81 Text: © 1994, Oxford University Press, Inc. Tune: From *The English Hymnal,* © Oxford University Press

82 Text: © 2000, GIA Publications, Inc.

83 Text: © 1994, Hope Publishing Co., Carol Stream, IL 60188. All rights reserved. Used by permission.

84 Text: © 1993, GIA Publications, Inc.

85 Text: © 1994, GIA Publications, Inc. Tune: Harm. from *The English Hymnal,* © Oxford University Press, Inc.

86 Text: © 1993, GIA Publications, Inc.

87 Text: © 1994, Selah Publishing Co., Inc., Kingston, NY 12401, www.selahpub.com. All rights reserved.

88 © 1972, Dawn Treader Music. Admin. by EMI Christian Music Publishing. International Copyright Secured. All Rights Reserved. Used by Permission

89 Text: © 1993, Kevin Mayhew, Ltd. Buxhall, Stowmarket, Suffolk, England. IP14 3BW. Used by permission.

90 © 1993, Howard S. Olson

91 Text: © 2000, GIA Publications, Inc. Tune: Harm. © 1938 (Renewed 1966) J. FISHER AND BRO. All Rights Assigned and Controlled by BELWIN-MILLS PUBLISHING CORP. (ASCAP) All Rights Reserved. Used by Permission.

Acknowledgements/*continued*

117 Text: From *A Singing Faith,* © 1984, Jane Parker Huber. Used by permission of Westminster John Knox Press.

118 Text: © 1996, Selah Publishing Co., Inc., Kingston, NY 12401, www.selahpub.com. All rights reserved. Tune: Harm. © 1938 (Renewed 1966) J. FISHER AND BRO. All Rights Assigned and Controlled by BELWIN-MILLS PUBLISHING CORP. (ASCAP) All Rights Reserved. Used by Permission.

119 Text: From *Hymns for Morning and Evening Prayer* by Aelred-Seton Shanley, © 1999 Aelred-Seton Shanley. Reprinted by permission of Liturgy Training Publications, Chicago Illinois

120 Text: © 1990, The Hymn Society. Administered by Hope Publishing Co., Carol Stream, IL 60188. All rights reserved. Used by permission.

121 Text: © 1991, Concordia Publishing House, Used with permission.

122 Text: © 1994, James Quinn, SJ. Used by permission of Selah Publishing Co., Inc., North American agent. www.selahpub.com. All rights reserved.

123 Text: © 1997, GIA Publications, Inc.

124 Text: © 1997, GIA Publications, Inc. Tuine: Harm. from *The English Hymnal,* © Oxford University Press, Inc.

125 Text: © Oxford University Press, Inc. Tune: © 1978, *Lutheran Book of Worship.* Reprinted by permission of Augsburg Fortress

126 Text: © 1997, GIA Publications, Inc.

127 Text: © 1982, Hope Publishing Co., Carol Stream, IL 60188. All rights reserved. Used by permission.

128 Text: © 1982, Jubilate Hymns Ltd. Administered by Hope Publishing Co., Carol Stream, IL 60188. All rights reserved. Used by permission. Tune: Arr. © 1989, Iona Community, GIA Publications, Inc., agent

129 Text: © 2000, GIA Publications, Inc. Tune: Harm. © 1938 (Renewed 1966) J. FISHER AND BRO. All Rights Assigned and Controlled by BELWIN-MILLS PUBLISHING CORP. (ASCAP) All Rights Reserved. Used by Permission.

130 Text: © 2000, GIA Publications, Inc.

131 Text: © 1991, Concordia Publishing House. Used with permission.

132 Text: © 1995, 1996, Sisters of St. Benedict, 104 Chapel Lane, St. Joseph, MN 56374-0220

133 Text: ©1990, Concordia Publishing House. Used with permission.

134 Text: © 1974, Hope Publishing Co., Carol Stream, IL 60188. All rights reserved. Used by permission.

135 Text: © 1997, GIA Publications, Inc.

136 Text: © 1990, Hope Publishing Co., Carol Stream, IL 60188. All rights reserved. Used by permission.

137 Text: © 1991, GIA Publications, Inc.

138 Text: © 2000, GIA Publications, Inc.

139 Text: © 1993, GIA Publications, Inc. Tune: © 1986, GIA Publications, Inc.

140 Text: © 1995, Selah Publishing Co., Inc., Kingston, NY 12401, www.selahpub.com. All rights reserved.

141 Text: © 1990, Hope Publishing Co., Carol Stream, IL 60188. All rights reserved. Used by permission.

142 Text: © 1997, GIA Publications, Inc.

143 Text: © 1997, GIA Publications, Inc.

144 Text: © 1998, GIA Publications, Inc. Tune: Harm. © 1984, Jack W. Burnam

Acknowledgements/*continued*

145 Text: © 2000, GIA Publications, Inc.

146 Text: © 1993, GIA Publications, Inc.

147 Text: © 1985, Oxford University Press, Inc. Tune: © Mrs. Alfred M. Smith

148 Text: © 1993, GIA Publications, Inc. Tune: Harm. from *The English Hymnal,* © Oxford University Press, Inc.

149 Text: © 1993, GIA Publications, Inc. Tune: © 1986, GIA Publications, Inc.

150 Text: © 1997, GIA Publications, Inc.

151 Text: © 1980, Hope Publishing Co., Carol Stream, IL 60188. Tune: © 1983, Hope Publishing Co., Carol Stream, IL 60188. All rights reserved. Used by permission.

152 Text: © 1994, Oxford University Press, Inc.

153 Text: © 1995, GIA Publications, Inc.

154 Text: © 1993, GIA Publications, Inc.

155 Text: © 1989, Hope Publishing Co., Carol Stream, IL 60188. All rights reserved. Used by permission.

156 Text: © 1970, Hope Publishing Co., Carol Stream, IL 60188. All rights reserved. Used by permission.

157 Text: © 1997, GIA Publications, Inc.

158 Text: Trans. © Peter J. Scagnelli

159 Text: © 1971, Hope Publishing Co., Carol Stream, IL 60188. All rights reserved. Used by permission.

161 Topical Index

Topical Index/*continued*

Topical Index/*continued*

Topical Index/*continued*

Title Index/*continued*